Praise for Wise Up! Experience the Power of Proverbs

I have two daughters, ages 12 and 13, and I'm so thankful for *Wise Up! Experience the Power of Proverbs*. Rebecca Ingram Powell knows the questions girls at this age are asking. More importantly, she knows where to find the answers and how to lead young women to the wisdom in God's Word. —Lisa Whelchel, Author, *Creative Correction*

Today, young women are bombarded with all kinds of media messages influencing them to do some really stupid things. Embracing godly wisdom is the only way our daughters are going to survive the plethora of temptations and peer pressures they will face. In this book, Rebecca brings the Proverbs to life and helps young girls "wise up" about a wide variety of issues and challenges. —Shannon Ethridge, Author, *Every Young Woman's Battle*

With cleverly compelling instruction grounded in richly biblical truths, Rebecca Ingram Powell illumines a faithful path for a girl's journey into womanhood. *Wise Up!* will grow young chicks into strong, soaring eagles. —Ginger Plowman, Author, *Don't Make Me Count to Three!*

Wise Up! is enjoyable, encouraging, and faith-stretching. Throughout the study, girls are presented with God's truth in a friendly, inviting, and applicable way. Studying Proverbs with *Wise Up!* feels like sitting down with a trusted friend who lovingly points out the paths of righteousness. —Bethany Notgrass, Director of the *amie* network

Each year I visit over 200 public high schools to speak and look into the faces of young men and women. Most young women are desperate for the wisdom and guidance to become strong and virtuous ladies. How do we help them? *Wise Up!* by Rebecca Ingram Powell is the perfect response. In nine weeks, a young woman can dive into the wisdom of King Solomon expressed in the Book of Proverbs. From journaling to scripture memory to a "passkey" that helps them unlock the lesson's truth, they will not leave this work unchanged. Rebecca has crafted a wonderful biblical study to bring wholesome transformation to young women! —Doug Herman, Author, *Time for a Pure Revolution*

Rebecca has an incredible gift of reaching the heart of the teen with a lesson that is memorable, challenging, and yet non-offensive and preachy. This study is incredible! —Cindy Rushton, Rushton Family Ministries

Wise Up!

Experience the Power of Proverbs

Rebecca Ingram Powell

Pleasant Word
A Division of WINEPRESS PUBLISHING

Layout design by Sherry Walker.
Printed in the United States of America.

Packaged by Pleasant Word, a division of WinePress Publishing, PO Box 428, Enumclaw, WA 98022. The views expressed or implied in this work do not necessarily reflect those of Pleasant Word, a division of WinePress Publishing. Ultimate design, content, and editorial accuracy of this work are the responsibilities of the author.

ISBN 1-4141-0399-9

Library of Congress Catalog Card Number: 2005900976

To Danya, my beautiful daughter.
You bring incredible
joy to my life. I love you.

Table of Contents

Foreword

Proverbs. The name invokes wisdom, a map for our lives. As mothers of teenage daughters, we need this counsel in abundance. Many of the issues our daughters are facing today are of such grave importance that how they respond to these can drastically change the course of their lives. They do not have the luxury of thinking they are exempt from worldly ways creeping into our Christian homes. They're exposed to them through publications, television, and friends—inside and outside the church. I believe Rebecca allowed the Holy Spirit to guide her as she wrote *Wise Up! Experience the Power of Proverbs*. Boldly, she discusses many of these issues as a mom sitting down with her daughter, firmly planting the Word of God in her heart. Enjoy this journey and embrace the changes with open arms as your own daughter grows and matures in the Lord.

Becky Longoria, Administrator
Aaron Academy
www.aaronacademy.com

Note to Parents

You've probably seen them at the mall. They are smothered in glittery eye make-up and chatting nervously through lips drenched in shiny gloss. Low-rise jeans hug skinny hips that are just beginning to develop a curve. Navels are exposed where too-tight shirts refuse to tuck in. These are today's girls. They think they want what the world has to offer. Sucked into a trap of premature sexuality by television, music, and their peers, they sell themselves short for temporary thrills.

It was no different twenty-five years ago, when I was twelve. In the mid-eighties, my friends and I wanted to be like Madonna and Pat Benatar. It seemed there was nothing more important than being cool. Unfortunately, cool wasn't defined as being the smartest girl in the class. Coolness rotated on an axis of physical beauty and sensuality, and it rested on the acquisition of a boyfriend. Times haven't changed.

Girls at the pivotal ages of 12 and 13 are making choices that will lay the foundation for their all-important teenage years. Despite the many advances made by our foremothers and the numerous opportunities available for women, most girls base their choices on the deception of a world that appeals to their flesh and their all-consuming need to fit in.

For several years, I have been praying for the Lord to guide me in a way to help my own daughter navigate adolescence. *Wise Up! Experience the Power of Proverbs* was created as a result of God's answering my prayers in a most unique way. *Wise Up!* is a Bible study curriculum for middle-school aged girls. It was written out of my heart's desire to provide my daughter, Danya, with a spiritual foundation during her early adolescent years. Like every American girl, she is being bombarded with the culture, and I wanted her to know the truth about our upside-down world. Even though we have homeschooled her from the beginning, the world wages an assault on our belief system every time we step out the front door, whether it's a trip to the mall or (sadly) just hanging around with the kids at church.

Having long been fascinated by the Jewish traditions of the bat mitzvah, I yearned for my daughter to experience a coming-of-age that would provide her with firm footing as she took those first steps into her teen years—exciting years that can be spent finding and following God's unique plan. *Wise Up!* is the answer to my prayers. This Bible study provides girls with foundational lessons that will pave the way into young womanhood. How will my daughter—and your daughter—keep her way pure? By living according to the precepts of God's Word.

Introduction

Welcome to a Bible study written just for you. *Wise Up! Experience the Power of Proverbs* is a nine-week, interactive study of the first nine chapters of the Old Testament book of Proverbs. Incredibly, King Solomon's straightforward instructions to his son concerning sex, friendships, finances, and good character are just as valid today. How can this ancient text apply to a girl your age, living in the 21st Century?

Actually, God's Word has a special quality that makes it different from anything else that has ever been written. In Hebrews 4:12, the apostle Paul explained that the Word of God is living and alive. It's inspired by the Holy Spirit. God uses Scripture to reveal His truth to us, and His truth never changes. So, what King Solomon taught his son about life and about people, about success and about failure, about priorities and about possessions, still makes sense today, thousands of years later.

My desire is for you to grow in God's truth and wisdom as you progress through this study. Please don't hurry through the lessons. Bible study should not be done in haste. Take your time. Eliminate any distractions by retreating to a quiet place. This is the most important part of your day. Don't cheat yourself out of the blessing of giving God your full attention.

Let me share with you the special features of this study.

Daily Bible Reading. *Wise Up! Experience the Power of Proverbs* begins each day with a brief Bible reading. Every week focuses on one chapter of Proverbs. Each day, you will read a portion of that week's chapter.

Proverbs Passkey. After you read, take a moment to focus on the Proverbs Passkey. A passkey is a master key, designed to open several different locks. In this Bible study, your <u>Proverbs Passkey</u> is simply the core of the day's lesson. Let God use this key verse to open your heart to the truths He has for you.

<u>Journaling.</u> You may already keep a diary or journal. Writing down your thoughts is a very healthy and comforting thing to do. When your life seems a bit too hectic, or when things are going on that seem a bit confusing, a journal can be a place where you sort things out. At the end of each day's lesson, you will find several questions. Answer the questions in complete sentences. Take the time you need to formulate your thoughts. And remember, you don't have to share these pages with anyone. You're not being graded on this! These questions are formulated in a way that will provoke you to deeper conversations with God. You're old enough now to be seeking the Lord on your own, and you must have a personal walk with Him to get through your teen years successfully. ***Wise Up! Experience the Power of Proverbs*** wants to help you do that by establishing the habit of a daily quiet time of Bible study and prayer, just you and God.

<u>Scripturistics.</u> Scripture memory is vitally important to your Christian life. Every day, take some time to work on this. This is explained fully in the pages of Appendix B.

<u>Password to Prayer.</u> A very important part of this Bible study is in the pages of Appendix C, ***Password to Prayer: A Perpetual Monthly Calendar of 31 Prayers for Girls.*** You may pray through these 31 prayers every month. These 31 prayers cover just about everything you can think of! Whatever the date is, pray the prayer that corresponds. For example, if today's date were November 6th, I would pray the 6th prayer at the end of my Bible study time. Tomorrow, I would pray the 7th prayer. There will be days when the prayer happens to fit exactly with your lesson, but there will be days when it doesn't. Just keep praying! You will be covering yourself with a holy armor as you present these petitions to God every month.

<u>Quotables.</u> Each lesson concludes with a quote from a remarkable Christian. Brief biographies of each person quoted can be found in Appendix A, along with websites and other resources.

Weekending. Friday is catch-up day. Use this day to read back over your journal entries, read through the entire chapter you've studied, and spend time thinking about what you've learned.

EXTRA! Each week has a little something extra that you can do to enhance your study. These are optional; however, they will give you even more opportunity to experience the power of Proverbs!

My prayer for you, young lady, is that you will focus on pursuing God through your teen years. These years are short, but they are bursting with choices. Let's study God's Word together and see just how beautiful your teen years can be when you choose Wisdom's ways over the ways of the world.

Unit One • Preview
The Beginning of Wisdom

Monday

Beginning Your Day: Your Personal Retreat

Tuesday

Beginning Your Relationships: How Important are Your Friends?

Wednesday

Beginning Your Teen Years: Wisdom's Cry

Thursday

Beginning Your Life's Planting: The Principle of Sowing and Reaping

Friday

Weekending

This Week's EXTRA!

Watch: *"Twice Pardoned: An Ex-Con Talks to Parents & Teens"*[1]

Monday • Lesson One
Beginning Your Day

Today's Passage

Read Proverbs 1:1-7

Proverbs Passkey

The fear of the Lord is the beginning of knowledge, but fools despise wisdom and discipline. Proverbs 1:7

Your Personal Retreat

What if your parents sat you down for a family meeting and explained that you were moving? And not to just any house, but to a home that is 55,000 square feet, with all kinds of maids and butlers? What if they told you that the reason you were moving was because your dad had a new job? And from now on, people would be calling him, "Mr. President."

When I was in the sixth grade, there was a girl my age who lived in the White House. Her dad was President Jimmy Carter. Her name was Amy. Amy was the first young person to live in the White House since John F. Kennedy's children. It seemed like it would be a lot of fun, but I don't think she liked it very much.

Whenever I saw pictures of Amy in the newspaper, she wasn't smiling. She had long blond hair and thick, round glasses. She was neither glamorous nor fashionable; she was just an ordinary girl who was getting a lot of attention that she probably didn't want. Everywhere she went, she was accompanied by Secret Service men. She was driven to school in a limousine. Cameras and reporters were always close by. It must have been difficult to be the President's daughter, especially at such an awkward time of growing up. Who wants the eyes of a nation watching when you're buying your first bra, or starting your period, or trying to figure out boys? Those are the days when a girl wants to be left alone.

Fortunately, Amy managed to find a getaway. Her parents had a tree house built for her on the White House grounds. It was a quiet, personal retreat for a growing girl. It was a place where she could go and think, or pray, or just be still.

Solomon, the writer of the book of Proverbs, was also the child of famous parents. His dad, King David, was the royal ruler of Israel. His mother was Queen Bathsheba. Solomon grew up to be the wisest man in the world because he asked God to give him wisdom. His proverbs, or "wise sayings," are a source of knowledge for people today. They will guide you through your growing up years, if you will study them and apply them to your life.

No matter who your parents are, it's hard to be a girl your age. This study is your chance to retreat every day and be with the One who knows you best and loves you most. Your Father in Heaven wants you to meet with Him daily. He wants you to know how beautiful you are, even if you don't feel very pretty. He wants you to know how special you are, even if you just want to be like everybody else. He wants you to know that He has wonderful plans for your life, even if you don't have a clue about what your future holds.

Decide on a place and time that you will work on these lessons each day. You might not have a tree house or even your own room, but perhaps you can find a spot somewhere that will suffice for a personal retreat. Ask your parents and siblings to respect your time alone with God.

Journaling

✻ Do you ever feel like everyone is watching you? What's the worst thing so far about growing up?

_____

_____

_____

_____

✻ What do your parents do for a living? Would your life be easier or more difficult if your parents were famous?

_____

_____

_____

_____

✻ Write down Proverbs 1:7. Use any translation you like. What do you think this verse means? Do you believe it? Do you think other people believe it?

_____

_____

_____

_____

_____

_____

_____

_____

✤ Name a person you know whom you think of as wise. Describe that person.

_____

_____

_____

_____

_____

✤ What is today's date? _____. Check Appendix C for your *Password to Prayer*.

Quotable

"The purpose of retreat is not to check off a list of Scriptures read, quotes studied, or prayers said. It is an escape into the calm arms of God." –Jane Rubietta

Tuesday • Lesson Two
Beginning Your Relationships

Today's Passage

Read Proverbs 1:8-19

Proverbs Passkey

My son [daughter], if sinners entice you, do not give in to them.
Proverbs 1:10

How Important are Your Friends?

Harold Morris was an all-star athlete in high school, headed for a successful athletic career. Yet it was only a few years later when he found himself serving two life sentences in the Georgia State Penitentiary. What happened? If you ask Mr. Morris today, he will tell you that he was hanging out with the wrong friends.

How important are your friends? According to Mr. Morris, your friends will determine the outcome of your life. That is a pretty strong statement. I have a feeling, though, that Mr. Morris is right.

When I was in middle school, my family moved from Nashville, Tennessee, across the state to Knoxville. I will never forget the first day at my new school. I didn't know a soul.

Everyone had to meet in the school auditorium. After the principal spoke, the students would be divided into classes and start the school day.

I dragged my mother into that auditorium with me. My mother is a school teacher, and she knows all about peer pressure. She knows what young people are feeling and thinking. When we walked in and sat down together, kids immediately started to chuckle and whisper because I had brought my "mommy" in to sit with me.

"Are you sure you want me to stay?" she whispered. I was sure! I didn't care what those others kids thought because I was scared to death. I knew I needed a friend.

It was a just a day or two later that I met Katie.[2] She became my best friend. We spent most of our time together. If we weren't in the same class, we would pass notes in the hall. Many afternoons, if she wasn't at my house, I was at hers. And then, of course, there were the **marathon phone** conversations every night. We told each other everything. Our friendship thrived because we stayed constantly connected.

By the time we were in high school, our circle of friends had expanded to include boys as well as girls. Katie had a crush on a guy who attended my church. That was all Rand* did—he just came to church with his parents. He wasn't a Christian, and he didn't love the Lord. Rand was playing around with drugs and alcohol. He didn't care about school. He didn't care about his life. He didn't care about anyone but himself. And my sweet friend Katie, well, Katie thought she was in love with him.

In the middle of our sophomore year of high school, Katie and her family moved two states away. Although we stayed in touch, our bond of friendship was severely weakened by the distance. In my mind, the day Katie moved to Ohio stands out as the absolute worst thing that happened to me in high school. The two of us could not understand why God was allowing it to happen.

A couple of years later, Katie and I got together during Christmas break. At that time, we had both completed the first semesters of our freshman years of college, Katie in a northern state and I in Murfreesboro, Tennessee. We sat on the floor in my parents' living room beside a beautifully decorated Christmas tree. After we exchanged gifts (Unknowingly, we had gotten each other t-shirts from our schools!), we started talking and laughing about old times together. Suddenly, Katie became quiet.

She absently raked her fingers through the carpet for a moment and then she looked at me in all seriousness. "Listen," she said earnestly. "I need you to know that moving was the very best thing that ever happened to me.

"If I had stayed here," she shook her head, "there's no telling what could have happened with Rand. I was so crazy about him that I would have done anything he wanted me to do. God moved me away to protect me. I know that now."

How important are your friends? The last I heard of Rand, he was working at a low-paying job. He never completed his education. While under the influence of drugs, he was involved in an accident. He suffered minor brain injury as a result. On the other hand, my friend Katie is a happily married mother of three. She completed her law degree, passed the bar, and today, practices law. *"Don't let anyone deceive you. Associating with bad people will ruin decent people."*[3]

Journaling

❋ Is it hard to say "no" to your friends?

_____

_____

❋ Proverbs 1:10 encourages us not to give in when we are enticed. To entice means to attract, persuade, or tempt. What are some things that you know tempt you? Can you come up with a plan for not giving in the next time those things attract you?

_____

_____

_____

_____

✴ List six qualities that you look for in a friend.

_____

_____

_____

_____

_____

✴ As you look over the six qualities that you listed, ask yourself which of the things you listed are traits that belong to *you*. Are *you* the kind of friend you're looking for? Be honest. What do you need to work on?

_____

_____

_____

_____

_____

✴ What is today's date? _____. Check Appendix C for your *Password to Prayer*.

Quotable

"The main quality to look for in a close friend is not how attractive, talented, wealthy, smart, influential, clever, or popular they are. It's how much they love and fear God."
–Stormie Omartian

Wednesday • Lesson Three
Beginning Your Teen Years

Today's Passage

Read Proverbs 1:20-27

Proverbs Passkey

Wisdom calls aloud in the street, she raises her voice in the public squares; . . . Proverbs 1:20

Wisdom's Cry

The book of Proverbs is all about how to make wise choices. Why does that seem to be such a difficult thing for people to do? Solomon wrote, "Wisdom calls aloud in the street, she raises her voice in the public squares." Solomon made the point that Wisdom longs to get our attention. God has not hidden the right way from us. On the contrary, He has underlined it, circled it in red, and drawn stars out beside it. *Here it is! This is the way to go!*

You may have played the game "Hot or Cold" with your friends. In this game, an object is hidden. The person who is "it" tries to find the object by listening to the other players tell her if she is "hot or cold." As she gets close to discovering the whereabouts of the object, she will hear, "Hot! You're getting hot!" However, if she begins to turn away from the object, or goes in a completely different direction from where it is located, she will hear, "Cold! Icy! You might as well be on the North Pole!"

When we follow God's laws, it is not difficult to determine the right way. He has spelled it all out for us in His Word. Plus, if you are a Christian, you have the benefit of the Holy Spirit living inside you. He acts as somewhat of an internal compass to keep you pointed in the right direction. Admittedly, it may not be so easy to actually DO the right thing! God presents us with choices every day of our lives. What we choose will decide the quality of our lives.

Journaling

※ Write down Proverbs 1:20. Use any translation you like.

_____

_____

_____

_____

※ How does wisdom "cry out" the obvious answer when it comes to smoking? Drinking? Doing drugs?

_____

_____

_____

_____

※ What are some ways that God has used to point you in the right direction?

_____

_____

_____

☀ Read "Why Memorize Scripture?" (Appendix B). Choose a passage to memorize. Write the reference of your selection, and tell why you chose this particular passage.

_____

_____

_____

_____

_____

☀ What is today's date? _____. Check Appendix C for your *Password to Prayer*.

Quotable

"Life is a series of choices between the bad and the good and the best. Everything depends on which we choose."
–Vance Havner

Thursday • Lesson Four
Beginning Your Life's Planting

Today's Passage

Read Proverbs 1:28-33

Proverbs Passkey

. . . they will eat the fruit of their ways and be filled with the fruit of their schemes. Proverbs 1:31

The Principle of Sowing and Reaping

The words "sowing" and "reaping" are words most girls today don't use very often. However, these terms are quite familiar to farmers and people who like to garden. When a person sows a seed, she is planting it. When that seed has produced, she "reaps" or harvests the crop it provided.

Let's say that you wanted a garden full of roses. Would you plant carrot seeds? Of course not! Sowing carrot seeds would only reap a garden full of delicious orange carrots. If you want roses, you must sow the right seeds.

Scripture tells us the principle of sowing and reaping applies to all of life. The apostle Paul explained this principle to the church at Galatia. He said, "Don't be misled: No one makes a fool of God. What a person plants, he will harvest. The person who plants selfishness, ignoring the needs of others—ignoring God!—harvests a crop of weeds. All he'll have to show for his life is weeds! But the one who plants in response to God, letting God's Spirit do the growth work in him, harvests a crop of real life, eternal life."[4] In other words, just as you can't plant carrot seeds and expect to grow roses, neither can you plant sin in your life and expect to harvest God's favor. God's blessing follows our obedience.

The principle of sowing and reaping is one of God's universal laws. Even the unbelievers in our world believe that you reap what you sow. A popular expression in today's world is, "What goes around, comes around." Most people believe that the way you treat other people is the way you yourself will eventually be treated. Sooner or later, a bully will wind up getting bullied by someone bigger and meaner. One day, the snob will get snubbed. And the person who makes jokes at the expense of others will find herself laughed at in the end.

What about the person who sows love?

The book of Ruth is about a woman who chose to sow love. Ruth was living in the middle of tragic circumstances. Her husband Mahlon had died, along with his brother and his father, leaving Ruth, her mother-in-law Naomi, and her sister-in-law Orpah widows. But Mahlon had not died without leaving Ruth an incredible gift.

Ruth was a Moabitess. Her hometown, Moab, was a heathen land that worshiped many gods. When Ruth met Mahlon and his family, she was introduced to Jehovah, the God of the Israelites. Mahlon, a Hebrew, gave Ruth the gift of the knowledge of God. Once Ruth began to learn about this God—the one, true God—she chose to serve Him. When the men of the family passed away and her mother-in-law Naomi decided to return to her homeland of Bethlehem, Ruth chose to go with her.

Ruth sowed love for her newfound God when she chose to accompany Naomi back to Bethlehem. She sowed seeds of selflessness in looking after Naomi's needs as though she were her very own mother. Ruth planted a crop of diligence as she went daily to the fields to gather grain so that she and Naomi could have something to eat.

What kind of harvest did Ruth gather? God blessed Ruth with an abundance. Not only did she remarry, but Ruth married the most honorable man in Bethlehem. Then the Lord gave her a baby boy! Even in her sorrowful situation, Ruth sowed seeds of love and obedience, and God produced a bountiful harvest in her life. In the thousands of years that the earth has existed, nothing has altered the principle of sowing and reaping. Nothing ever will.

Journaling

Sow a thought, reap an act;
Sow an act, reap a habit;
Sow a habit, reap a character;
Sow a character, reap a destiny.
–Aristotle

♥ Copy the above quote by Aristotle.

_____

_____

_____

_____

♥ Why is it difficult to develop good habits, but easy to fall into bad ones?

_____

_____

_____

_____

_____

_____

_____

_____

♡ Is there a good habit that you would like to develop? Think through and list the steps necessary to sow it into your life.

_____

_____

_____

_____

_____

♡ Work on your passage for memorization.

♡ What is today's date? _____. Check Appendix C for your *Password to Prayer*.

Quotable

"Proverbs gives us a long list of sins that get us into trouble, such as impatience, dishonesty, selfishness, a hot temper, and even talking too much. It also tells us that wisdom will keep us out of trouble. Anytime we ignore God's principles, we eventually suffer the consequences. We always reap what we sow." –Rick Warren

Friday • Lesson Five
Weekending

Today is your day to:

❀ Complete any unanswered questions from this week's lessons.

❀ Read back through Proverbs 1 and your journal entries for this week.

❀ Do some soul-searching about what God is teaching you. Record your thoughts below.

_____

_____

_____

_____

_____

❀ Copy the Scripture you are memorizing on a separate sheet of paper.

❀ What is today's date? _____. Check Appendix C for your *Password to Prayer.*

❀ Watch this week's **EXTRA!** *"Twice Pardoned: An Ex-Con Talks to Parents & Teens."*

Unit Two • Preview
Facets of Wisdom

Monday

Parental Wisdom: Listening to Love and Experience

Tuesday

Protective Wisdom: His Presence in the Storm

Wednesday

Discerning Wisdom: When the Buzzer Goes Off

Thursday

Life Wisdom: The Walk of the Righteous

Friday

Weekending

This Week's EXTRA!

Check out *The Facts of Life and Other Lessons My Father Taught Me* by Lisa Whelchel. You may also want to visit her website: www.lisawhelchel.com. Ask your mom if she remembers this TV show.

Monday • Lesson One
Parental Wisdom

Today's Passage

Read Proverbs 2:1-8

Proverbs Passkey

. . . for he guards the course of the just and protects the way of his faithful ones. Proverbs 2:8

Listening to Love and Experience

Growing up, there were plenty of times that I had disagreements with my parents, but one time in particular stands out in my memory.

I was almost eleven, and a teen celebrity, Leif Garrett, was coming to town. He was coming as part of a promotional event for a local radio station. The station held a Walk-a-thon every year for charity, and Leif was going to participate. This young man's face was plastered all over my walls. He had been my "heartthrob" for months. I was dying to meet him and eagerly making plans to take part in the event. Was I concerned about the charity that was raising money through the Walk-a-thon? No, in fact, I don't even remember which charity it was. I just wanted to meet Leif Garrett.

Here's the problem: the Walk-a-thon was going to be held on a Sunday, beginning at eight o'clock in the morning. There was somewhere else that I was supposed to be on Sunday mornings. My daddy was a preacher, and my family was in church every Sunday. When I approached my mom and dad with my plan, they vetoed it immediately. There was no way I was going.

I fussed. I pouted. I locked myself in my room. I put up signs on my door about needy children who would have to do without the money I could have raised in the Walk-a-thon. Did they change their minds? No.

Sometimes it's difficult to understand why parents do the things they do. In today's Scripture reading, however, we find wise King Solomon pleading with his son to accept his commands. More often than not, parents' instructions come from their life experiences. Your parents have been around a lot longer than you have. They have made lots of mistakes and learned from them. As a little girl, you believed them when they told you not play with matches or touch a hot stove. Believe them now.

When my daughter Danya was three years old, we went to the mall and wandered into a store that sold clocks. The shop we were in had some very expensive, antique watches and other timepieces behind a glass case. Danya went over to look at the glass case, and then for some reason, she began to bang on the glass. I quickly got her away from it and explained to her that the glass was breakable. I told her that she could get hurt if the glass were to shatter.

Had she ever seen a broken piece of glass? No.

Did she know that glass was fragile and easily destroyed? Not until I told her.

Did she have any clue how much it would cost me if she broke it? None at all.

I knew the glass could break. I had seen broken glass; indeed, I had broken a small glass figurine in a store when I was her age. My three-year-old Danya trusted me when I told her not to bang on the glass. She obeyed me.

It took a while for me to come around to my parents' decision about the Walk-a-thon, just as it may take you a while to come around to the decisions your parents make for you today. Things aren't quite so cut and dried as they were when you were three. In my case, I realized that I wanted to take part in this charity event not because my heart had a passion for the needy, but because my heart had a passion for the celebrity. What I needed was a passion for God and His Church. That's where my place was, not chasing some stringy-haired boy around town. My parents knew that my time would be better spent at church. Today, twenty-five years later, I know they were right. (And since you've never heard of Leif Garrett, you know they were right, too!)

Journaling

❋ Can you think of some other reasons why my parents wouldn't let me go to the Walk-a-thon?

_____

_____

_____

_____

❋ What do you do when you disagree with your parents? Do you react in a godly manner? What should you do?

_____

_____

_____

_____

_____

✽ Look at Proverbs 2:4. How can you compare your parents' instruction to a "hidden treasure"?

_____

_____

_____

_____

_____

✽ Work on your passage for memorization.

✽ What is today's date? _____. Check Appendix C for your *Password to Prayer*.

Quotable

"Children, obey your parents in the Lord, for this is right. 'Honor your father and mother' – which is the first commandment with a promise – 'that it may go well with you and that you may enjoy long life on the earth.'" –St. Paul

Tuesday • Lesson Two
Protective Wisdom

Today's Passage

Read Proverbs 2:9-15

Proverbs Passkey

Discretion will protect you, and understanding will guard you. Proverbs 2:11

His Presence in the Storm

One spring night when I was a little girl, a terrible storm came whipping through Nashville. At that time of year, serious thunderstorms can hit middle Tennessee, often developing into tornadoes. In our neighborhood there was a power outage, and unfortunately, we didn't have a battery-powered radio. During severe weather, people are advised to seek shelter in an underground basement or in the innermost part of a building, away from windows. Since we didn't have a basement, my parents, my sister, and I had gathered in the hallway, the safest place in our house, to wait out the storm.

We crouched together there, listening to the squalling wind outside. I couldn't see anything, and I hated that. I think I was more scared of the dark than of the storm! I started to wonder if Momma and Daddy were really there in the hallway with us. I got very still and quiet. I could hear the storm raging all around, but somehow, above the storm, I could hear my dad's steady breathing, calm and assured. I couldn't see him, but I knew that he was there. I could feel him. His presence was strong and comforting, and even though he didn't say anything, I knew that everything was going to be all right.

Finally, it seemed that the winds were dying down. My mother asked Daddy, "Well, what should we do now? There's no telling when they will get the power back on."

Daddy replied, "Let's pray and then go to bed. It's late—already past the girls' bedtime." We bowed our heads together. Daddy prayed for protection from the storm. He asked God for a good night's rest. He just prayed a simple, trusting prayer. Then he and Momma helped my sister and me find the way to our beds. We went to sleep in the middle of the storm as rain continued to pelt the roof and lightning danced outside.

When we awoke the next morning, my family went through the usual morning routine of eating breakfast and getting dressed for school. It wasn't until we got in the car and began backing out of the driveway that we even realized the effect of my dad's faith-filled prayer.

As we looked through the car windows at our neighborhood, we saw that during the night, trees—huge weeping willow trees—had been uprooted. Up and down the street, their huge trunks lay like flatlines in people's yards. The giant hand of the storm had ripped the trees from the ground. Some roads were impassable. From homes and vehicles to mailboxes and street signs, storm damage was everywhere. It was everywhere, that is, except at our house. Our home was fine; our lawn was neat; our yard displayed, incredibly, a clearly marked boundary of prayer.

God's Wisdom offers you the benefit of knowing what to do in the middle of a storm. The passage you read for today explains that our God gives wisdom, knowledge, and understanding. He is our guard through the storms, and He is also our guide. We are protected by our Lord.

Does that mean that life will be easy? No.

Does that mean that nothing bad will happen? No, not necessarily. What it means is that we can trust the Lord to be there, beside us, no matter what.

You may not be able to see Him.

You may not hear Him saying anything. You may only be able to hear the storm raging all around you.

However, if you get very still and quiet, you will be able to feel His presence. You will hear the whisper of His breath above the howling winds, and you will *know* He is there.

Journaling

✳ What are you afraid of?

_____

_____

_____

_____

_____

_____

✳ Can you remember a time when God protected you from danger?

_____

_____

_____

_____

_____

_____

✳ Are there times when you don't *feel like* God is with you? What would you tell a friend who said, "I don't think God cares about me"?

_____

_____

_____

_____

_____

✳ Work on your passage for memorization.

✳ What is today's date? _____. Check Appendix C for your *Password to Prayer*.

Quotable

"But seek first the kingdom of God and His righteousness, and all these things will be provided for you." –Jesus Christ

Wednesday • Lesson Three
Discerning Wisdom

Today's Passage

Read Proverbs 2:16-19

Proverbs Passkey

None who go to her [the adulteress] return or attain the paths of life. Proverbs 2:19

When the Buzzer Goes Off

My friend Wendy was a cute, outgoing blond with a knack for making friends. Her bubbly personality captivated everyone she met. As a college student, Wendy enjoyed going to night clubs with her friends. Her enthusiasm for life showed in her lively moves on the dance floor. Wherever she went, Wendy always got the attention of the club's band members, and her circle of friends was forever growing.

When Wendy became a Christian, the Holy Spirit moved into her heart and began to show her that certain things were hindering her Christian life. Determined to pursue Christ, Wendy quit drinking. When she told her friends about her decision, she noticed that only a few of them supported the choice she had made. Rather than lose friends, she began to keep quiet about her life with Christ. She didn't think God would want her to quit having fun, so she continued going out with her friends on the weekends. She became the "designated driver" so she could have an excuse for not drinking and be sure her friends got home safely.

This arrangement seemed like it was going to work for Wendy. She was able to have fun and go dancing with her friends, and she didn't bother them with the details of her new life with Christ. One day, however, Wendy came to me with a serious question.

"Rebecca," she said, "I just don't feel right when I go out with my friends anymore. They talk about things that I'm not interested in, and they don't want me to talk about the Lord. I want to have fun, but it's not fun anymore. What's going on?" As I pressed Wendy for more details, she shared that she felt the most uncomfortable when her friends in the band played a song they had written. It was a crowd favorite, but the song was full of obscene language—a foul message repeated over and over.

I knew that the Holy Spirit would bless Wendy with a spirit of **discernment** if she would only ask for it. What is **discernment**? Author Neil Anderson explains:

> **Discernment**…[is] that "buzzer" inside, warning you that something is wrong. For example, you visit someone's home and everything appears in order. But you can cut the air with a knife. Even though nothing visible confirms it, your spirit detects that something is wrong in that home.
>
> The first step to understanding discernment is to understand the motive which is essential for employing [using] it. In 1 Kings 3:9, Israel's king Solomon cried out to God for help. God answers: "Because you have asked this thing and have not asked for yourself long life, nor have asked riches for yourself, nor have you asked for the life of your enemies, but have asked for yourself discernment to understand justice, behold, I have done according to your words. Behold, I have given you a wise and discerning heart" (verses 11, 12). The motive for true discernment is never to promote self, to amass personal gain, or to secure an advantage over another person— even an enemy… **Discernment has one primary function: to distinguish right from wrong.**[5]

"Wendy," I said, "ask God to show you what is really going on in that club. He will."

The next time Wendy went to the night club, she quietly bowed her head and asked God to show her the truth about the club and whether or not it was okay for her to be there. When she lifted her head, she saw a murky black cloud filling up the room. No one else noticed its suffocating presence. Wendy watched as the entire room was covered by a blanket of blackness. After a few seconds, the inky darkness faded away. Wendy told me that she recognized immediately that God was showing her the presence of evil in the room.

You may not have an experience as dramatic as Wendy's, but there are many times when you will hear that "buzzer" going off in your heart. Will you listen to God when He prompts you to make good choices? When the buzzer goes off, be obedient. God has big plans for your life.

Journaling

☀ Have you ever heard the "buzzer" go off? What happened?

_____

_____

_____

_____

_____

_____

_____

_____

☀ Are there any people or places that make you feel uncomfortable? Do you think that God is trying to tell you something?

_____

_____

_____

_____

☀ What would you tell Wendy about her friends?

_____

_____

_____

_____

_____

☀ Work on your passage for memorization.

☀ What is today's date? _____. Check Appendix C for your *Password to Prayer*.

Quotable

"Discernment is not a function of the mind; it's a function of the Holy Spirit which is in union with your soul/spirit. When the Spirit sounds a warning, your mind may not be able to perceive [or make out] what's wrong. Have the courage to acknowledge that something is wrong when your spirit is troubled." –Neil Anderson

Thursday • Lesson Four
Life Wisdom

Today's Passage

Read Proverbs 2: 20-22

Proverbs Passkey

For the upright will live in the land, and the blameless will remain in it; . . . Proverbs 2:21

The Walk of the Righteous

Growing up, I was a big fan of the television show, "The Facts of Life." It was a cute, funny show about middle school-aged girls who went to boarding school together. I wasn't the only person who liked it. It was one of the most popular sitcoms of the Eighties. Lisa Whelchel was one of the stars of the show.

Like most sitcoms that run for several years, "The Facts of Life" began to lose some of its punch in its last few seasons. The girls themselves were all growing up. Original cast members had started to leave. The show was coming to a close. In an effort to revive it, however, the producers decided that in the show's last season, it was time for one of the characters to lose her virginity. After all, the show was called, "The Facts of Life," yet sex was a topic they had never fully explored.

I remember hearing a news brief on the radio when the announcer made mention of this upcoming episode. He also announced the newsworthy item that Lisa Whelchel, the young actress who played the character Blair Warner, had refused to participate in this show because of her Christian beliefs.

It's one thing to be known for being wholesome, but to take an honest, authentic position for Christ is quite another. I could hardly believe it! Here was a beautiful TV star speaking out for Christ! I was so impressed with that. It made an impact on my life to discover that Whelchel was a Christian and that she was not afraid to stand up for what she believed.

I never forgot that incident. A few years ago, Lisa Whelchel returned to the spotlight after a decade of marriage and motherhood. This time, she wasn't acting; she was releasing a couple of Christian books and talking about her life as a homeschooling mother of three. I purchased her autobiography and eagerly skimmed through it, hoping to find a passage where she talked about her decision not to appear on that particular episode of "Facts of Life." I was not disappointed. Here is what she said in her book, *The Facts of Life and Other Lessons My Father Taught Me*:

> In the original script for that episode, Blair was to take a stand for abstinence. That was extremely gracious of the producers, but I requested to be written out of the episode altogether. Although it would have been a wonderful opportunity to share the truth about the value of waiting for marriage to have sex, it would have been offered as just another option, not as God's perfect plan. I realized that the overall message of the show would perpetuate the lie that having sex before marriage is natural, with no negative consequences as long as people practice "safe sex."

The path of the righteous, mentioned today in your Scripture reading, is not the easiest road to take. It requires a certain boldness from us as Christians. In our world, whenever anyone takes a stand for the Lord, she is immediately in the spotlight, whether on a national scale or simply among her circle of friends. That's not easy, but doing the right thing isn't always easy or popular. Wisdom teaches, however, that when we follow the path of righteousness—the road less traveled—it leads us to the powerful blessings of God. This makes all the difference in our lives, and it makes a difference in the lives of others, as well. Cherish this poem by Robert Frost. Read it aloud. I hope it becomes one of your favorites.

The Road Less Traveled

Two roads diverged in a yellow wood
And sorry I could not travel both
And be one traveler, long I stood
And looked down one as far as I could
To where it bent in the undergrowth

Then took the other as just as fair
And having perhaps the better claim
Because it was grassy and wanted wear
Though as for that, the passing there
Had worn them really about the same

And both that morning equally lay
In leaves no step had trodden black
Oh, I kept the first for another day!
Yet, knowing how way leads onto way
I doubted if I should ever come back

I shall be telling this with a sigh
Somewhere ages and ages hence
Two roads diverged in a wood
And I took the one less traveled by
And that has made all the difference

Journaling

♡ Copy the last stanza of "The Road Less Traveled" here.

_____

_____

♥ Why was presenting abstinence as one of several options not good enough for Lisa Whelchel?

_____

_____

_____

_____

♥ What are some ways that God asks Christians to take the road less traveled? What will you do when He asks you to do something that is not easy?

_____

_____

_____

_____

♥ Work on your passage for memorization.

♥ What is today's date? _____. Check Appendix C for your *Password to Prayer*.

Quotable

"The consequences [of premarital sex], regardless of the outcome, impact a person's life forever. Once a girl gives away her virginity, she can never get it back. God created sex, and He instructs his children to wait until marriage to enjoy it."
–Lisa Whelchel

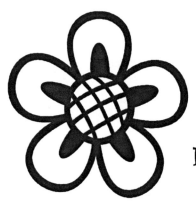

Friday • Lesson Five
Weekending

Today is your day to:

❀ Complete any unanswered questions from this week's lessons.

❀ Read back through Proverbs 2 and your journal entries for this week.

❀ Do some soul-searching about what God is teaching you. Record your thoughts below.

_____

_____

_____

_____

_____

❀ Work on your Scripture memory passage. You can do it!

❀ What is today's date? _____. Check Appendix C for your *Password to Prayer.*

❀ Don't forget this week's **EXTRA!** Check out *The Facts of Life and Other Lessons My Father Taught Me* by Lisa Whelchel. You may also want to visit her website: www.lisawhelchel.com.

Unit Three • Preview
Wisdom along the Way

Monday

In All Your Ways: Acknowledging God

Tuesday

The Pleasant Ways: Paths of Peace

Wednesday

Out-of-the-Ways: Bypassing the Drive-Thru

Thursday

Neighboring Ways: Making a Difference

Friday

Weekending

This Week's EXTRA!

Do something out of your way for a neighbor, family member, or friend. It doesn't have to be anything fancy. Make some muffins, write a note, or sweep a front porch.

Monday • Lesson One
In All Your Ways

Today's Passage

Read Proverbs 3:1-8

Proverbs Passkey

Trust in the Lord with all your heart and lean not on your own understanding; in all your ways acknowledge him, and he will make your paths straight. Proverbs 3:5,6

Acknowledging God

One of my favorite episodes of the classic sitcom, *The Andy Griffith Show*, is entitled, "My Fair Ernest T. Bass." Andy and Barney decide to teach the backwoods, redneck, hillbilly Ernest T. how to be a true gentleman. Barney takes it upon himself to show Ernest T. how a sophisticated, cultured man enters a room upon arriving at a social function. Barney role-plays walking in the front door. He removes his hat, tucking it under his arm. He proceeds around the empty room, pretending to greet everyone with a handshake, a smile, and mouthing (lip-syncing) a few kind words. Okay, it might be a stretch, but the point is that Barney *acknowledges* everyone in the room.

What does it mean to acknowledge? The online Merriam-Webster dictionary defines *acknowledge* with several meanings:

1 : to recognize the rights, authority, or status of

2 : to disclose knowledge of or agreement with

3 a : to express gratitude or obligation for **b** : to take notice of **c** : to make known the receipt of

4 : to recognize as genuine or valid

This dictionary further explains the word in this way, "*Acknowledge* implies the disclosing of something that has been or might be concealed."

Our relationship with God and our faith in Him are things that we might be able to conceal. Think about it. We don't have to let on that we are Christians. If you get too much money back from a cashier, you can cleverly conceal Christ's effect on your life by simply keeping the change. When your friends are making fun of someone you don't like anyway, you can hide God's love by going along with it. Those times when your siblings are really getting on your nerves, you can completely bury your Christian witness by blowing your top. But be warned: If we don't acknowledge God, we aren't admitting His presence in our lives. If we don't admit His presence, we limit His power.

Think of all the "rooms" in your life: ♥ Family room ♥
♥ Neighborhood room ♥ Home room ♥ School room ♥
♥ Church room ♥ Sports room ♥ Hobby room ♥ Friends room ♥

When you walk into these rooms, do you acknowledge God? I am not talking about verbally confessing to every person you pass by, *Hey! I'm a Christian!* St. Francis of Assisi said, "Preach always; when necessary, use words." We can acknowledge the presence of God by our attitude, our actions, and our admission—in the everyday details of our lives—that we belong to Christ. Sometimes we will use words. Sometimes we won't.

For years, Judge Roy Moore of Alabama kept a hand-carved wooden plaque of the Ten Commandments hanging outside his office door. He believed that the Lord had put him in the office of judge, and he chose to honor God and acknowledge Him in this way. Some time later, Judge Moore chose to once again publicly acknowledge his faith and his allegiance to Almighty God by erecting a 5,200 pound granite monument of the Ten

Commandments in the rotunda of the Alabama state Supreme Court building.

Judge Moore was asked to remove the monument. Initially, he refused because his interpretation of the Constitution provided him the freedom to display the Ten Commandments. However, after many court battles and appeals, along with a national controversy, the monument was indeed removed. But Judge Moore acknowledged God. I believe the Lord God acknowledges Roy Moore, too. He is blessed among men for what he did in taking a stand for the Lord.

It's not going to be easy to *acknowledge* God in all of your ways. The world and culture you live in wants to deny the presence of God. Jehovah is a bother and an inconvenience to a selfish society that lives to cry out, "Me first!" However, you can change your corner of the world. Begin by practicing today. As you enter every room of your life, take off your hat, smile, and offer words of praise to the Lord who loves you and wants you to know He is there. When you acknowledge Him, He promises to make your paths straight. He will keep you on track!

Journaling

❊ Copy these sentences: "If we don't acknowledge God, we aren't admitting His presence in our lives. If we don't admit His presence, we limit His power."

_____

_____

_____

_____

_____

✳ When is it easy to acknowledge God's presence?

_____

_____

_____

_____

✳ Whether you acknowledge God or not, He is always present. Have there been times in your life when you tried to ignore God, but deep in your heart, you knew He was still there? How did you feel?

_____

_____

_____

_____

_____

✳ Work on your passage for memorization.

✳ What is today's date? _____. Check Appendix C for your _Password to Prayer_.

Quotable

"I ran across the Ten Commandments that I had carved by hand some ten years earlier. I would have been quite hypocritical not to acknowledge the One who had placed me in office, so I hung them on the wall. I knew they would be controversial, but I did not suspect this would become a national controversy." –Alabama Chief Justice Roy Moore

Tuesday • Lesson Two
The Pleasant Ways

Today's Passage

Read Proverbs 3:9-18

Proverbs Passkey

Honor the Lord with your wealth, with the firstfruits of all your crops; . . . Proverbs 3:9

Paths of Peace

I re-read the letter from our friends Marc and Carol. They were serving as missionaries to students on the campus of my alma mater. Marc and Carol did an awesome job of sharing Christ with college kids and discipling them, one by one. Theirs was a powerful ministry that I was thankful to support. At the time, Rich and I sent them $25 every year. It wasn't a lot of money, but we were newly married. After our regular tithe, we didn't have a lot to spare. The note they had sent us was their yearly newsletter, detailing what God had been doing through their campus ministry. Twenty-five dollars didn't seem like much to give. I wanted to give more.

I was pregnant with my first baby and working a temporary job. My husband and I planned for me to stay home once she was born. Our tight budget was about to get even tighter, but still, I longed to give a larger gift to Marc and Carol. As missionaries, they were totally dependent on the financial generosity of others for their support. "God," I prayed, "I want to give Marc and Carol a bigger gift this year. I wish I could give them something like $300!" How crazy was that? I guess it was just crazy enough for me to pray this: "Lord, if You'll give me $300, I will give it to Marc and Carol."

A few days later, my boss came to me with some unexpected news. For the past couple of months that I had been working at this office, my paychecks had been miscalculated. The company owed me some money. How much? Guess. You're right. I received a check for approximately $300.

Now, here's what I hate admitting. I sent that money straight to Marc and Carol, but as I was putting it in the mailbox and raising the flag for it to be picked up, I began to struggle. I thought of our empty nursery and all the things that we needed for our new baby. I thought of the doctor and hospital bills that $300 would certainly help pay. And I hesitated. Then, fortunately, I remembered: I asked God for $300 to give to our friends in ministry. He provided it. This money was never mine. I closed the mailbox door and ran back up the stairs to our apartment.

It's no coincidence that today's Scripture reading begins with instructions to tithe and ends with the assurance of peace. Money is an area that can be a source of chaos or a place of peace in your life. I believe that the key to the direction it will take for you lies in your ability to understand that your money does not belong to you. Ultimately, all income and gifts come from God. They don't belong to us. We are called to be managers, or stewards, of the money that is entrusted to us. How could I give away money that we could have obviously used ourselves? Because I knew that money wasn't mine.

You may be familiar with the principle of tithing. God calls us as His children to give Him ten percent, or a tithe, of what we have. Do we do this because God needs our money? No. We give back to God as a way to honor Him. When we give back, we are showing our appreciation. We are recognizing that all we have comes from Him. The other ninety percent of our money belongs to God just as much as the first ten percent. We are to manage it wisely.

When Danya was born, she came home to a nursery filled with every good thing. Rich and I were showered with gifts from friends and family in such abundance. We didn't have to buy anything for her! Our needs were met in an incredible way by our Heavenly Father.

I received a letter from Marc several weeks after sending the check. He had been hoping to attend a conference for further mission training. He was short $300. Rather then worrying about it, he had trusted God to provide the money if he was supposed to go to the training conference. The check God had me send came just in time. When we trust the Great Provider, we will walk a path of peace.

Journaling

※ Why do you think it is difficult for people to maintain an attitude of peace when it comes to money?

_____

_____

_____

_____

_____

※ How can you avoid money worries as you grow up?

_____

_____

_____

_____

✳ Ask your parents or grandparents to tell you about a time in their lives when God miraculously provided for their needs. Record what they say here.

_____

_____

_____

_____

_____

✳ Work on your passage for memorization.

✳ What is today's date? _____. Check Appendix C for your *Password to Prayer*.

Quotable

"If we view giving as something that takes away from what we want, then we'll never experience joy in giving. But if we view our giving as a kingdom investment, our whole perspective changes." –Lysa TerKeurst

Wednesday • Lesson Three
Out-of-the-Ways

Today's Passage

Read Proverbs 3:19-26

Proverbs Passkey

My son [daughter], preserve sound judgment and discernment, do not let them out of your sight; they will be life for you, an ornament to grace your neck. Proverbs 3:21

Bypassing the Drive-Thru

Remember the Bible story of the twin brothers, Jacob and Esau? Esau was born first, if only by a few minutes. That guaranteed him the special privileges and advantages that belonged to a Jewish child who was the first-born son, among those, the birthright.

The birthright was a holy, sacred gift, determined by birth order, which was determined by God. It included receiving a double portion of the father's inheritance. The birthright could actually be withheld or transferred, usually at the father's discretion. No son in his right mind would ever do such a thing, until Esau. Esau transferred his birthright to his brother Jacob. He traded it, in fact, for a bowl of stew.

The Bible tells us that Esau had been hunting in the country all day. He had returned home absolutely famished. Jacob had been working around the tents all day and had a nice pot of soup simmering. Esau asked for a bowl of the stew. Jacob, well aware of the potential of his brother's ravenous appetite, answered, "First, give me your birthright."

Just what went through Esau's mind when Jacob presented him with this "deal"? How did Esau make his choice? And why?

Most people make choices based on three factors:

- Convenience,

- Habit, and

- Appearance.

These factors can work independently, or they can combine to create a more powerful influence. For example, the success of the drive-thru window is due largely to convenience, habit, and appearance working together. It is extremely **convenient** to pick up a sandwich. Millions of people pick up a breakfast sandwich every day on the way to work; thus, it becomes a **habit**. The drive-thru has a beautiful, full-color sign, and the parking lot is clean. The window itself is sparkling. It has a pleasant **appearance**.

Most people don't stop to think about the consequences of their choices. In the case of the daily drive-thru customer, she isn't thinking about the fact that her tasty bacon, egg, and cheese biscuit has 31 total fat grams, 250 mg of cholesterol, and 1360 mg of sodium. This adds up to a poor health habit that will not be convenient when it manifests itself in physical problems later on.

Esau made a poor choice. He sabotaged his own future when he got swept up in the here and now of a whining, grumbling stomach. He reasoned angrily, "Look! I am about to die! What good is the birthright to me?" Was he really about to die? No. Was the birthright going to be a lot of good to him? Yes. But convenience, habit, and appearance got the best of Esau.

Jacob made Esau swear an oath to him, and the deal was made. The pact was permanent. A lasting trade of eternal significance changed Esau's life. What did he get in return? A bowl of lentil stew, or POTTAGE, a cheap, common food of no value. (The term pottage is used as slang in India to refer to anything that is worthless.) You could say that Esau traded his birthright for the convenience of ancient Middle Eastern junk food.

Our choices affect our lives on a daily basis. We choose what we are going to wear, what we are going to eat, and what we are going to watch on TV. We choose whom we are going to call, whom we are going to befriend, and whom we are going to avoid. We choose how we are going to act, how we are going to speak, and how we are going to treat our family members. In making our daily choices, let's be careful to take them step-by-step and bypass the drive-thru.

Journaling

☀ What are some important decisions that you've made so far in your life?

_____

_____

_____

_____

_____

_____

_____

_____

_____

_____

_____

_____

_____

_____

☀ In a way, you have a birthright because of choices your parents have made. For example, my parents haven't left me land, cattle, and sheep, but they have given me the riches of a Christian home. They chose to love the Lord and love each other. What is your birthright?

_____

_____

_____

_____

☀ Work on your passage for memorization.

☀ What is today's date? _____. Check Appendix C for your *Password to Prayer*.

Quotable

"One woman and the choices she makes can go on to impact this world for centuries to come." –Mary Farrar

Thursday • Lesson Four
Neighboring Ways

Today's Passage

Read Proverbs 3:27-35

Proverbs Passkey

Do not withhold good from those who deserve it, when it is in your power to act. Proverbs 3:27

Making a Difference[6]

By Mike Griffin

(The following recollection is written by Mike Griffin and excerpted from *A Woman's Secret to a Balanced* Life by Lysa TerKeurst and Sharon Jaynes.)

I remember that hot August Day in 1961. My cousins, my sister, and I spent most of the summer at our grandparents' house. There were six of us in all, ranging in age from about three to ten. Our parents would leave us with Grandma while they went to their jobs during the day. My grandparents didn't have much, but we never really knew the difference. To us, our grandparents' house was a wonderful place where we were loved and accepted and cared for, albeit quite simply.

And we thought that old house on 22nd Street was a magical place. It had an old basement where we could play Hide-and-Go-Seek, an enormous tree that was perfect for climbing, and a large grassy field where we played baseball. What more could a kid want?

Air conditioning was experienced only in the large department stores or during the occasional adventure to the movie theater. It was hot, and the heat was something that on those summer days could drain even six energetic kids.

As we lolled about the house, a tapping at the screen door rattled the stillness. It might be a door-to-door salesman! In those days salesmen carried large suitcases filled with brushes or pots and pans or some other new gadget. We all knew our grandma had no money to buy the stuff they were selling, but it was fun to watch the man pull out all those neat brushes and brooms and show how they could "clean up the house in half the time." On very rare occasions, that tap at the door might be an uncle or an aunt who had a car and was offering to take us to get ice cream.

We all raced to the door. None of us was prepared for what we saw. A little woman was standing there. We were just kids, but we could tell by looking at her that she had seen hard times, very hard times. Her face was wrinkled, and her shoulders were hunched over. I remember most of all the expression on her face and in her eyes. It was as if she didn't want to see anymore. Even at the age of nine, I knew that to be the look of hopelessness. Her simple dress was patched and frayed. Her shoes had holes.

Behind her stood a little girl, maybe six or seven years old. She was dirty from following her mother about those hot streets. She had no shoes. She had no smile. I remember her hair being matted to her forehead by the sweat, which made little brown lines as it dripped through the dust on her face.

"Is your mother home?" the little lady asked in a weary voice.

"No, but my grandma is," replied my cousin, and off she ran to find Grandma.

The rest of us stood there at the door staring. We said nothing. We all wanted to do something, but we didn't know what to do.

Grandma soon hurried to the door, drying her wet hands in her apron as she walked. She pushed open the screen door and peered through her bifocal glasses at our visitors. Before Grandma could speak, the little lady reached into a brown paper bag and pulled out a red foil package. She opened the foil pouch revealing sewing pins and needles.

"Would you like to buy some pins?" she asked.

Grandma, somewhat surprised, her eyesight not the best, squinted to get a better look at the little girl and finally replied, "How much are they?"

The lady replied, "Oh, anything you can give me."

Now, we knew Grandma had no money. It took all of Grandpa's hard-earned paycheck just to cover the bills and buy the groceries. She went to the closet, and we all followed, wondering what she would do.

We watched her pull out her big, black, Sunday pocketbook. She dug in every little pouch and pocket and turned it upside down and shook it. She found one dime and two pennies in a crease in the bottom. Going back to the kitchen, she pulled out a large brown paper grocery bag. She filled it up with cans of tomato soup, potatoes, tomatoes, and beans from her garden, and biscuits she had made for supper.

She tucked a doll into the bag, carefully hiding the toy beneath the food. She had kept the doll, which had belonged to one of her children, on the mantle above the fireplace. And she had made a beautiful dress for it with leftover pieces of material from her sewing projects. We knew this doll was special to her; none of the girls ever played with "Grandma's doll."

Grandma went back to the front door and gave the lady the bag of groceries and the twelve cents. She said, "This is all I have. Please take it, but please don't make me take your pins."

"Thank you, ma'am," said the lady, barely able to speak. She turned and walked down the blistering street with the little girl silently following, but we barely saw them. We kids were watching our grandmother. We knew when she had her eyes closed and her mouth was moving quietly that she was praying. She acted as if she were watching the little family walk down the hill, but we knew she was praying for them.

We were in awe of our grandmother. Even at our young age, we knew we had witnessed what Jesus had said, "She has given more than all the others. She has given all she had."

Journaling

♥ What touches you the most about this story?

_____

_____

_____

_____

_____

_____

_____

_____

_____

_____

_____

♥ The narrator of this story, Mike Griffin, seems most affected by the fact that his grandma gave away her special doll. Why do you think Grandma wanted to give her doll to that little girl?

_____

_____

_____

_____

_____

♥ What is your most special possession? Would you be willing to give it away if God asked you to?

_____

_____

_____

_____

_____

♥ Work on your passage for memorization.

♥ What is today's date? _____. Check Appendix C for your *Password to Prayer*.

Quotable

"You can give something. Somehow, giving reminds us that the world does not revolve around us and that no matter what our financial status is, someone always is in a much worse situation." –Dave Ramsey

Friday • Lesson Five
Weekending

Today is your day to:

❀ Complete any unanswered questions from this week's lessons.

❀ Read back through Proverbs 3 and your journal entries for this week.

❀ Do some soul-searching about what God is teaching you. Record your thoughts below.

_____

_____

_____

_____

_____

❀ Work on your Scripture memory passage. You can do it!

❀ What is today's date? _____. Check Appendix C for your *Password to Prayer.*

❀ Don't forget this week's **EXTRA!** Do something out of your way for a neighbor, family member, or friend. It doesn't have to be anything fancy. Make some muffins, write a note, or sweep a front porch.

Unit Four · Preview
Wisdom Takes the Gold

Monday

No Deposit, No Return: The Cost of the Crown

Tuesday

Practice Makes Perfect: An Unlikely Olympian

Wednesday

Cheaters Never Prosper: Wisdom Wins First Place

Thursday

It's How You Play the Game: A Gracious Victor

Friday

Weekending

This Week's EXTRA!

Do some further research on Olympian Wilma Rudolph. There are several videos and books available. Check your local library.

Monday • Lesson One
No Deposit, No Return

Today's Passage

Read Proverbs 4:1-9

Proverbs Passkey

Wisdom is supreme; therefore get wisdom. Though it cost all you have, get understanding. Proverbs 4:7

The Cost of the Crown

If you have ever watched the Olympic Games on television, you may have seen the thrilling moment when the winner is presented with a gold medal for first place. Second and third place winners also receive medals (silver and bronze). All three athletes then stand before the crowd while the winner's national anthem is played. Even viewing this moment from my living room, I am still deeply moved as I imagine what the winner must be feeling. All those years of sacrifice and dedication have paid off.

When the gold medalist is interviewed by the television commentators, you quickly learn that the winning was not left up to chance. You will never hear a champion casually saying that her sport is a hobby or something she does in her spare time. Whether on an ice rink, on a race track, or in a swimming pool, every winner has one thing in common: she has given her life in pursuit of the gold. What could possibly motivate a person to make that kind of trade?

John Naber captured five medals (four gold and one silver) at the 1976 Olympics. A competitive swimmer, Naber broke four world records that year. Here is his story.

I was enjoying a bottle of root beer from an ice-filled Styrofoam chest. When I pulled out the glass bottle, the label came off but four words remained visible which taught me a life-changing lesson.

The words said simply, "No Deposit, No Return."

To enjoy the flavor inside, I had to pay the price. I had to invest in my dreams, if I wanted to see those dreams come true. I'm certain the maker of that bottle was thinking something else, but to this impressionable eleven year old, the words carried a lot of weight. I thought to myself, what am I depositing, in order to see my dreams come true? What price am I willing to pay?

Every Olympian feels the same way. It is the act of paying the price "up-front," the willingness to invest in ourselves, the understanding that we have to feel tired in order to get stronger, which has allowed us to reach the medal platform. Some call it delayed gratification. I call it common sense.

In the course of my career, (swimming ten miles per day, six days per week, eleven months a year) I traveled the equivalent of twice around the planet's equator. Each winter morning I walked across an ice-covered cement deck, steam rising from the pool's surface, bleeding the top three inches of water of their treasured temperature. The first swimmer in the pool (usually me) was the "ice-breaker" stirring up the water for the guys who followed. They often teased me about my eagerness because I sprinted the warm-up, crammed the "free-swim" periods with thousands of yards and was often the last one out of the pool.

Viewed from the perspective of a deposit or an investment, the long hours in a pool or weight room were no longer a punishment, sacrifice, penalty or even an inconvenience. The hours spent now seemed like an investment in my future.[7]

In your Scripture reading today, King Solomon admonishes his sons to get wisdom and pursue understanding, "though it cost all you have." Have you ever considered that godliness comes with a price? Of course, salvation is God's free gift to us. Jesus Christ paid the price for our sins so that we wouldn't have to. But godliness—becoming a truly godly young woman—is costly.

Jesus said, "Don't look for shortcuts to God. The market is flooded with sure-fire, easygoing formulas for a successful life that can be practiced in your spare time. Don't fall for that stuff, even though crowds of people do. The way to life—to God!—is vigorous and requires total attention."[8]

Journaling

✳ Look up Jeremiah 29:13 and copy it here.

_____

_____

_____

_____

_____

_____

✳ An Olympic champion has sought the gold medal with her whole heart. How can you give your whole heart to pursuing God?

_____

_____

_____

❀ What could your church do and be if everyone made an Olympian commitment to pursue Wisdom? Think about this and write a 5-7 sentence answer.

_____

_____

_____

_____

_____

_____

_____

_____

_____

❀ Work on your passage for memorization.

❀ What is today's date? _____. Check Appendix C for your *Password to Prayer*.

Quotable

"Once we've decided to pay the price and to say, 'Yes, Jesus, whatever it costs, I choose to obey,' we'll find out in the end it really cost us nothing because all we wanted was Jesus anyway." –Heather Mercer

Tuesday • Lesson Two
Practice Makes Perfect

Today's Passage

Read Proverbs 4:10-17

Proverbs Passkey

When you walk, your steps will not be hampered; when you run, you will not stumble. Proverbs 4:12

An Unlikely Olympian

Wilma Rudolph was born in a tiny Tennessee town in 1940. She was the seventeenth of nineteen children. As a child, Wilma lived with poor health. She contracted double pneumonia and scarlet fever. Later, Wilma's body was diagnosed with polio. Her left leg began to atrophy, or weaken and deteriorate. Doctors told her family that Wilma would never walk again.

Although the doctors sent Wilma home wearing an iron leg brace, they didn't realize they were sending her home to a mother who didn't believe in the word "can't." The Rudolphs refused to believe the doctors. They determined that Wilma would walk again.

Wilma and her mother took a 50-mile bus trip twice a week to the nearest hospital that would treat African-Americans. After receiving physical therapy, Wilma went home and practiced on her own. Everyone in the large family took turns each day massaging Wilma's leg and helping her with exercises. Wilma's mother told her that with faith in God, the leg brace would one day come off. Wilma believed in God, and she believed in herself.

After spending two years bedridden, Wilma took her first step on her own when she was nine years old. By the time she was eleven, the leg brace came off.

What did Wilma do when she was finally set free from her limitations? She began to run. It was slow at first, but with practice and persistence, she soon began to run with the passion that had lain dormant in her heart for so many years. She lost many races, coming in last place, before she finally began to come in second to last. It wasn't long before Wilma was winning every race she ran.

In his book, *Something to Smile About*, Zig Ziglar writes, "At age 15, just four years after she threw away the brace, [Wilma] was invited by Ed Temple to train with the Tigerbelles, the celebrated Tennessee State University women's track team. At age 16, she qualified for the 1956 Olympic team but won only a bronze medal. She then enrolled at Tennessee State on a track scholarship and trained under Ed Temple, who coached the 1960 Olympic team. On that team Wilma became a superstar. On the day before her first heat in the 100, she severely sprained her ankle but still won gold medals in the 100 meter and the 200 meter. She then anchored the 400-meter relay en route to her third gold medal."

Wilma was blessed to have a mother who knew the value of godly wisdom. She knew that with God, nothing is impossible. She knew that her daughter could walk again with the Lord's help. She committed herself to encourage and assist her daughter, daring her to believe in a God she could not see or hear or touch. The apostle Paul wrote in the book of Hebrews, "Now faith is being sure of what we hope for and certain of what we do not see."[9] What Wilma could see was a mangled, withered leg. She could have put her trust in the doctor's hopeless diagnosis of a life spent crippled. Wilma chose to follow wisdom. She put her faith in a God whose healing hand she could not see, and Wilma Rudolph became an unlikely Olympian—the first woman to win three gold medals.

Wilma's story inspires me to believe that with practice, persistence, and passion, my dreams can come true and my deepest hopes can become reality. What are you dreaming of?

Journaling

❋ What if Wilma's mother had not encouraged her to have faith in God?

_____

_____

_____

_____

❋ "You've got to put feet to your faith." What do you think this old saying means? How did Wilma and her family put feet to their faith?

_____

_____

_____

_____

_____

_____

_____

❋ You have dreams of your own. Write down one of your dreams here. Make a list of steps you need to take to reach your goal.

_____

_____

_____

_____

_____

_____

_____

_____

_____

_____

_____

_____

_____

_____

❋ Work on your passage for memorization.

❋ What is today's date? _____. Check
   Appendix C for your *Password to Prayer*.

Quotable

*"What Wilma Rudolph did was incredible! I believe her
success was not in spite of her problems, but because of them.
She treasured the good health that others took for granted.
Her joy filled her with an exuberance that intensified her training
and enabled her to outshine the athletes of her day. Think about it.
Follow your star, and chances are good you will reach new heights." –Zig Ziglar*

Wednesday • Lesson Three
Cheaters Never Prosper

Today's Passage

Read Proverbs 4:18-19

Proverbs Passkey

The path of the righteous is like the first gleam of dawn, shining ever brighter till the full light of day. Proverbs 4:18

Wisdom Wins First Place

In 1988 there was quite a scandal at the Olympic Games. Runners Carl Lewis (American) and Ben Johnson (Canadian), long time rivals, were pitted against each other in the 100 meter race. Canada said that Ben Johnson was the fastest man in the world. The United States made that claim about Carl Lewis. They had raced each other a total of fifteen times before the '88 Olympics held in Seoul, Korea. Carl had won nine of those competitions, and Ben had won six. As the young men lined up at the starting blocks, Americans held their breath to see who would win.

The winner was Ben Johnson. That day, the Canadian ran faster than any man in history. He ran 100 meters in 9.79 seconds. He broke every record that had ever been set. He was the fastest man in the world.

Two days after his victory, Ben Johnson was asked by the Olympics committee to take a drug test. He tested positive for drugs being in his system. He had been using steroid injections, carefully monitored by his trainer and a personal physician, to improve his performance. Ben's trainer, a man whom he trusted, had talked with him about using drugs to enhance his speed. He encouraged Ben, who was tired of being beaten by Carl Lewis time after time, that taking the steroids would give him the edge he needed to win. Ben decided to do it. He knew that drug use was illegal and that if he was ever caught, he would face severe punishment by the International Olympic Committee. Yet, knowing the risk, he took a chance—all for the sake of winning the gold.

Ben's coveted gold medal along with his record-breaking victory was stripped from him and given to Carl Lewis, who had come in second. Ben Johnson lost upwards of thirty million dollars in commercial endorsements. He was accused of betraying his country and became the butt of jokes—his name forever associated with "cheater" rather than "champion."

What motivated Ben Johnson to risk everything? Was it the money? Was it the fame? Was it the glory of winning? He pursued winning with passion, but for him, he was willing to win in name only, knowing that he himself didn't win but that a chemical substance had won the race for him. What kind of a champion is that?

Wisdom calls us to the life of an AUTHENTIC champion. After all, Jesus is the real thing, and He calls us to a life of authenticity as well. There are plenty of people out there who are willing to be known for something they are not. As Christians, however, we are called to a life of character, not simply reputation. Someone once said, "Reputation is what others think of you. Character is who God knows you really are."

A champion friend won't cheat by breaking promises.

A champion daughter won't cheat by disobeying her parents.

A champion sister won't cheat by embarrassing her siblings around others.

A champion wife won't cheat by flirting with other men or dreaming about long-lost boyfriends.

A champion student won't cheat by copying off someone else's paper.

I spent most of my middle school and high school years sitting behind Mark Hayden*. Teachers seated us alphabetically, so I always wound up behind Mark. When we were freshmen in high school, for some reason, my English teacher seated us in reverse alphabetical order. Mark ended up sitting behind me. This gave Mark a clear view of my paper one day when we were taking a test. What I didn't know was that Mark was cheating off me. What Mark didn't know was that I had totally misunderstood the concept we were being tested on. Normally a straight-A student in English, that day I missed every answer on the quiz. Mark was so upset when he got a zero that he begin to rant and rave. "I can't believe this!" he fussed, pointing at me. "The day I decide to cheat off her is the day she gets a zero!"

Cheaters never prosper. Eventually, they are found out. Scandal follows, as does shame. Victory comes when the gold is rightfully handed to the authentic champion.

Journaling

☀ Whom do you think of as an authentic Christian? (This needs to be a person that you know.) List some of this person's character qualities. Which of these qualities do you need to work on in your life? Ask God to help you.

_____

_____

_____

_____

☀ What might have been going through Ben Johnson's mind when they came to take the gold medal away from him?

_____

_____

_____

_____

_____

☀ How do you think that Carl Lewis felt when he was given the gold medal?

_____

_____

_____

_____

_____

☀ What is today's date? _____. Check Appendix C for your *Password to Prayer*.

Quotable

"Circumstances may appear to wreck our lives and God's plans, but God is not helpless among the ruins. God's love is still working. He comes in and takes the calamity and uses it victoriously, working out His wonderful plan of love." –Eric Liddell

Thursday • Lesson Four
It's How You Play the Game

Today's Passage

Read Proverbs 4:20-27

Proverbs Passkey

Above all else, guard your heart, for it is the wellspring of life.
Proverbs 4:23

A Gracious Victor

My son Derek was five years old when he started playing baseball. One day I asked him, "What is it you love most about baseball?"

He grinned and said, "When we say, 'Bad game! Bad game!'"

Puzzled, I asked him, "When do you say that?"

"Mom," he sighed, "at the end of the game. You know, when we all go out on the field."

"When you line up to shake hands with the other team?" I prodded.

"Yes," he replied. "That's when we all say, 'Bad game! Bad game!'" He was grinning from ear to ear. I hated to ruin the whole thing for him, but I could feel a lecture rising up inside me. I knew we needed to chat about this. Derek was referring to the traditional goodwill team walk. It provides closure to the game and is supposed to be a sportsmanlike gesture on the part of both teams.

"Derek," I said, "did you know that you were supposed to be saying, 'Good game!' to the other players?"

"Mom," he sighed again, "we all know that."

Then I understood. I guess when you're a five-year-old baseball player, the stress and confusion of the real game is not nearly as fun as your own hand-slappin', trash-talkin' tradition at the end.

The summer of 2002, my family eagerly watched the United States team from Kentucky win the Little League World Series. I cheered enthusiastically for the incredible kids who had played their hearts out. We Powells felt a real connection with the team from Louisville because of our own Kentucky ties (and American pride, of course!). We felt like we got to know those boys and their coaches. After all, even a child is known by his doing.

When Kentucky's pitcher Aaron Alvey realized his team had just won the Little League World Series, it was the greatest moment of his life. In this game alone he had homered for the game-winning run. In the series itself, he set two pitching records for strikeouts and scoreless innings and tied the mark for consecutive no-hit innings. He was the victor! At the age of 12, he was sitting on top of the world.

I had seen the camera panning across the dugout where the Japanese team was sobbing uncontrollably. What would happen when those players were lined up for the traditional goodwill team walk? Would they be able to extend their congratulations to the American winners? What would the Americans do when they saw all those tears?

Aaron Alvey led the Kentucky team to the field. I noticed a flicker of concern cross his young face when he found he was looking straight into a sea of wet, Asian eyes — a mob of little boys whose heaving mouths bawled the choking cries of their defeat. In what I believe to be an even greater moment of victory for Aaron Alvey, I watched as he reacted by doing something genuinely sportsmanlike and generously compassionate. Rather than only extending his hand, Aaron Alvey opened his arms. He hugged the Japanese players and patted their backs with careful respect. However exuberant he and his teammates felt inside, they showed a gracious humility when they realized their victory came at a heartbreaking price for the team that lost.

Such is the type of modesty displayed by a compassionate victor. Most of the time, this kind of winner has seen plenty of losses in her own life, and she knows well how to be sensitive to others. I'm sure that's why God allows losses in our lives. That's why He allows defeat, embarrassment, pain, and loneliness. These trials prepare us to minister to others. When the victories come along, as they most certainly will, we must never forget there are those on the perimeter who are suffering from sorrow.

Journaling

♥ "I knew we could go somewhere, but I didn't think we could go this far," said Aaron Alvey after winning the Little League World Series. We've been talking about your dreams this week. You know you can go *somewhere*. Commit to God your highest hopes and dreams. Spend some time journaling about how you want to "play the game."

_____

_____

_____

_____

_____

_____

_____

_____

_____

_____

_____

_____

_____

💗 Look up 2 Corinthians 1:14 and copy it here.

_____

_____

_____

_____

💗 Work on your passage for memorization.

💗 What is today's date? _____. Check
   Appendix C for your *Password to Prayer*.

Quotable

*"Circumstances have been placed in my life for the
purpose of cultivating my character and conforming me to
reflect Christ-like qualities. And there is another purpose.
Second Corinthians 1:14 explains it in terms of our being able to
comfort others facing the same kinds of trials."* –Joni Eareckson Tada

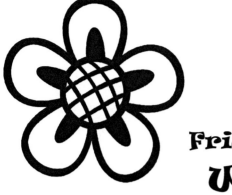

Friday • Lesson Five
Weekending

Today is your day to:

❀ Complete any unanswered questions from this week's lessons.

❀ Read back through Proverbs 4 and your journal entries for this week.

❀ Do some soul-searching about what God is teaching you. Record your thoughts below.

_____

_____

_____

_____

_____

❀ Work on your Scripture memory passage. You can do it!

❀ What is today's date? _____. Check Appendix C for your *Password to Prayer*.

❀ Don't forget this week's **EXTRA!** Do some further research on Olympian Wilma Rudolph. There are several videos and books available from your local library.

Unit Five · Preview
Wisdom Issues a Warning

Monday

Warnings of the Heart: Reality Check

Tuesday

Warning Signs: Staying Inside the Lines

Wednesday

A Word of Warning: Sex Has a Price Tag

Thursday

Warning Bell: Sounding the Alarm

Friday

Weekending

This Week's EXTRA!

Visit your local crisis pregnancy center. Call ahead to let them know you are coming. Take a gift of diapers, wipes, or baby formula with you.

Monday • Lesson One
Warnings of the Heart

Today's Passage

Read Proverbs 5:1-6

Proverbs Passkey

For the lips of an adulteress drip honey, and her speech is smoother than oil; but in the end she is bitter as gall, sharp as a double-edged sword. Proverbs 5:3,4

Reality Check

(Note: The Scripture for today, in fact, the entire fifth chapter of Proverbs, deals with adultery. As you read, keep in mind that Proverbs was written by a father for his son. Don't take it is as a personal slam against the female sex that the king admonishes his son against loose women. There are plenty of loose men about whom a king's daughter must be warned. Rearrange it in your mind so that you read the warnings as your own caution against guys who are not pursuing the Kingdom!)

We were folding clothes in the laundry room of our dorm. It was a quiet Friday night, and anyone who lived within an hour of MTSU had already gone home for the weekend. The moist room smelled pleasantly of detergent and fabric softener. A gentle breeze drifted in the windows, creating just the right temperature. My friend Michelle* and I were enjoying the luxury of having all the washers and dryers available for our own personal use. We were talking, laughing, and enjoying snacks from the vending machine when suddenly, Michelle began to cry.

"What's wrong?" I asked, bewildered. Shaking her head, Michelle grabbed my hand, and we began running down the hall to her dorm room. She flung open her door and tore a calendar from her bulletin board. She shoved it in front of my face. Even in my confusion, I noticed that she had circled a date, two weeks before, in red ink. "What's this all about?" I asked.

"Don't you see?" she hissed through her tears. "Don't you see? I was supposed to start my period two weeks ago! I'm pregnant!"

The memory today is as real to me as when it happened then. I could not have been more shocked. Michelle was one of my best friends and a good, Christian girl. Her boyfriend was devoted to Christ as well, with plans to go into the ministry. How could something like this have happened?

The dictionary defines *adultery* as sexual intercourse between a married person and someone other than his/her spouse. The Bible takes the definition of adultery a step further, however, and defines it as any unlawful sexual intercourse. This would include *fornication*, or sex between unmarried people, as well.

Studies have shown that Christian young people are just as likely to participate in sex before marriage as non-Christian young people. Surprised? I think I may have a clue as to why.

For Christian young people, drinking and drugs may be easier sins to avoid because they take some planning. When you're underage, you really have to do some planning in order to get your hands on alcohol. And illegal drugs, well, that would take some setting up as well. But sex? Usually people say that it "just happened." They didn't plan it. Somehow both people wind up naked, and it just happens? Of course not!!! That is just ridiculous. It's not that they planned for it to happen. It's that they didn't plan for it *not* to happen.

If you plan on not taking drugs, then you won't hang around with people who do. If you plan on not becoming an alcoholic, then you won't even take the first drink. If you plan on remaining pure for your husband, then you will begin now building hedges (more on hedges tomorrow) around your virginity in order to preserve it.

The next week, Michelle got a pregnancy test at a local clinic. She was definitely expecting, and she and her boyfriend decided to get married. Michelle hadn't planned to get married while still in school. She hadn't intended to have a child while she herself was so young. She had other plans, goals, and dreams for her life. She was a bright student who had looked forward to enjoying an education, a college degree, and an exciting career doing something she loved.

I love babies! But babies are a lot of work. And a single woman's, or teen's, unplanned, unexpected pregnancy is not God's best way of doing things. God created families to take care of babies. Remember Solomon's admonition: *You don't want to squander your wonderful life!* You have a wonderful life! You do! Don't let some stupid, selfish guy talk you out of it— even if you think you love him. Love Jesus more. Just love Jesus more.

Journaling

❋ Rebecca St. James defines "true love" as being willing to wait for sex. Do you agree or disagree with her? Do you have a definition of true love? Write down God's definition of true love, John 3:16. Use more than one Bible translation—at least two—and copy it several times below.

_____

_____

_____

_____

_____

_____

_____

_____

_____

_____

_____

_____

_____

_____

_____

❋ Work on your passage for memorization.

❋ What is today's date? _____. Check Appendix C for your *Password to Prayer*.

Quotable

"We don't need to settle for second best, and that's something I share in concert: Live God's way because His way is the greatest way. His way rules. Don't get messed up in the junk that so many people get messed up in. I've had so many people come up to me and say, 'I got involved with drugs and alcohol, and I had sex outside of marriage, and I regret it now.' Don't get involved with the junk. Live for God. Wait for God's best. I'm willing to wait for a husband who will love me as Christ loved the church, somebody that will truly love me. And if he truly loves me, he's going to be patient, and he's going to wait for me, and he's going to want me to wait, too. That's true love." –Rebecca St. James

Tuesday • Lesson Two
Warning Signs

Today's Passage

Read Proverbs 5:7-14

Proverbs Passkey

Keep to a path far from her, do not go near the door of her house, lest you give your best strength to others and your years to one who is cruel, . . . Proverbs 5:8,9

Staying Inside the Lines

When I was a little girl growing up in Nashville, Tennessee, I remember watching my dad as he took great care of our yard. We had a roomy corner lot, and Daddy took an artistic pride in the many shrubs and bushes that were on our property. A beautiful, lush, green hedge separated our yard from our next door neighbor's, and I remember the many times I watched my Daddy work on it. This was long before electric gardening tools became available. My dad used a large pair of manual hedge clippers, and he barbered those bushes with skilled expertise! They were perfectly crafted by the time he was finished, cut in perfect boxes with magnificent ninety-degree angles on every side. Daddy's hedges hemmed in the boundaries of our yard. They defined the perimeters of our property. But the pride he took in them caused them to be more than mere margins—they were masterpieces!

Jerry Jenkins (you may know him as the author of the *Left Behind* book series) believes that hedges need to be erected in our lives in order to create boundaries around our sexual purity. This goes for teens as well as adults, single people as well as married couples. We set up our boundaries, or limitations, and then we tend to them. We take pride in them. Now is the time to decide where to plant your hedges.

God's Word is a great place to start. The Bible makes it clear that sexual sin, whether it's before marriage (fornication) or after marriage (adultery) is wrong. Take a look at this contemporary paraphrase of 1 Corinthians 6:16-20.

> There's more to sex than mere skin on skin. Sex is as much spiritual mystery as physical fact. As written in Scripture, "The two become one." **Since we want to become spiritually one with the Master, we must not pursue the kind of sex that avoids commitment and intimacy, leaving us more lonely than ever — the kind of sex that can never "become one."** There is a sense in which sexual sins are different from all others. In sexual sin we violate the sacredness of our own bodies, these bodies that were made for God-given and God-modeled love, for "becoming one" with another. Or didn't you realize that your body is a sacred place, the place of the Holy Spirit? Don't you see that you can't live however you please, squandering what God paid such a high price for? The physical part of you is not some piece of property belonging to the spiritual part of you. God owns the whole works. So let people see God in and through your body.[10]

Hedge number one should be saving sex for marriage.

Unfortunately, you are living in a sex-crazy world. The American culture is totally obsessed with sex. And fornication, or sex before marriage, is totally accepted by our sinful society. In fact, as you get older, you will find that the approval of fornication is one of Satan's most widely accepted false teachings. Sex before marriage is okay, he says. Everyone does it. And indeed, it does seem like everyone does, but that's not true.

If you listen to secular radio stations and music by groups that aren't Christian, then you will probably hear a lot about sex. Watching television shows and even the commercials could also lead you to believe that everyone is having sex without the benefit or commitment of marriage. But keep in mind, those songs and TV shows are godless. There is no mention of God, so why should there be any adherence to His laws?

It's easy to sin if you don't know any better. If the enemy can get people to believe there is no God, then he can soon have them believing there is no such thing as sin. If there is no wrong, no evil in the world, then there is no need for a Savior, right? And if there is no need for Jesus, then salvation is a fairy tale and Christianity is just a theory. Once God is introduced and recognized, however, sin doesn't come as easy. Conviction follows, and the need to get back in harmony with God becomes an all-consuming goal.

As Paul explains in the passage from 1 Corinthians, sexual sin is in many ways different from other sins. Sex involves your body, your mind, and your emotions. Sexual sins linger; you carry them with you into adulthood. The least of these consequences would be unpleasant memories and bitter regrets. The worst would be contracting sexually transmitted diseases that can lead to infertility (being unable to bear children) or even death.

Plant your hedges. It's never too early. As you plant them, keep in mind that they must be carefully tended. One of my hedges as a teenager was to never date a boy who was not a Christian. A boy came along whom I thought was absolutely great, and he told me he was a Christian. Sadly, his actions didn't back up his words.

If you ever find your hedges growing out of control, it's time to do some clipping. Cut things and people out of your life that cause your boundary lines to become blurry. Your life is wonderful! The hedges you plant out of obedience to God are beautiful. God will bless you through your hedges. I promise!

Journaling

❋ Write down a few hedges you want to plant around your sexual purity. Ask God to bless your hedges and make them a beautiful witness of His love.

_____

_____

_____

_____

_____

_____

_____

_____

_____

_____

❋ Work on your passage for memorization.

❋ What is today's date? _____. Check Appendix C for your *Password to Prayer*.

Quotable

"Why [is] it so important that people not commit adultery? I submit that the reasons, whatever they are, are the same reasons we need to build hedges around our hearts, eyes, hands, spouses, and marriages. If adultery is in the same class as murder, it is a threat not only to our marriages but to our very lives." –Jerry Jenkins

Wednesday • Lesson Three
A Word of Warning

Today's Passage

Read Proverbs 5:15-20

Proverbs Passkey

May your fountain be blessed, and may you rejoice in the wife of your youth. Proverbs 5:18

Sex has a Price Tag[11]

By Pam Stenzel

You won't believe what I discovered during the nine years that I counseled girls who came into my pregnancy counseling offices in Chicago and Minneapolis. Most were worried sick about being pregnant. Very few were concerned about the venereal disease epidemic that is sweeping America.

Girls would come to my office and say: "Pam, if I had known this was going to happen to me, I would have made a different choice. But no one told me." I began to ask these girls: "What could we have told you? What could someone have shared with you, before you made your choice?" After all those years I realized there are a lot of students making decisions about sex who have no idea what the consequences of their decisions will be. I am writing this so that none of you will ever again be able to say to a physician, a counselor, or to your future husband or wife: "Nobody told me. I didn't know."

Girls Hope They're Off The Hook. Most teens who are having sex are afraid of getting pregnant. Girls come into my office for pregnancy testing, and when I tell a girl her test is negative, she gets a look of relief over her face, as though to say: "I'm off the hook. I'm not pregnant. Let me out of your office." Wait a minute! Have you been tested for syphilis, gonorrhea, herpes, chlamydia, trichinoma, vulvadema, urethritis, hepatitis B, HPV or HIV? **You have a four times greater chance of contracting a sexually-transmitted disease than you do of becoming pregnant.**

For nine years I've also had to tell hundreds of girls their tests were positive — "You're pregnant." Immediately they want an easy, painless way out. I have to look at them and say: "Sorry. Your choices at this point are bad, terrible, and worse. You had a good choice before you chose to have sex. Now all of your choices are going to carry painful lifelong consequences."

Abortion, Anorexia, Bulimia, Suicide. There is no easy way out of pregnancy. Abortion is painful, destructive, and devastating. More than 80 percent of the women in our country who've had an abortion say that if they could go back, they would have chosen something different. Abortion isn't like going to the dentist and having a tooth pulled. I have counseled with hundreds of women—five, ten, fifteen years after they had an abortion—who are still hurting physically, psychologically, and above all, spiritually. I've counseled teenagers with anorexia, bulimia, and depression — including many who have attempted suicide because they had an abortion.

Parenting a child isn't an easy choice either. Eight out of ten single teenage girls who choose to parent their children will live below the poverty level for at least ten years. Most stay there the rest of their lives. Nine out of ten will never attend college. These are girls who had goals, plans, things they might have liked to do with their lives after high school that they didn't get the chance to do because of their rash choice to have sex.

Venereal Disease Epidemic. Today, in the next 24 hours, 12,000 teenagers will contract a sexually transmitted disease (STD). And that's just teenagers. Looking at the entire population, there are about **50,000 people each day** in our country who contract a sexually transmitted disease. Yesterday, 12,000 of them were teenagers who got up in the morning like some of you reading this, and said: "It's not going to happen to me. That happens in big cities, but not where I live." Wrong!

Chlamydia Sterilizes. In the 1950s there were only five sexually transmitted diseases that were known and treated. Today there are more than *fifty* types of STDs. Chlamydia is the number one STD among teens today. There are about 4,000 teenagers every day who contract chlamydia. This is a bacteria, not a virus.

Unlike some venereal diseases, it can be cured. But more than 80 percent of the students who contract this disease do not realize they have it. If you contract chlamydia once in your life, you have a 25 percent chance of being sterile the rest of you life. If you get this disease more than once, the chances are much greater that you will never be able to have children.

At first, abstinence may sound negative, but it's a very positive choice that brings you freedom and peace of mind. Sex is not a game. But if you treat it like a game, it can have very harmful, long-term consequences. Sex was meant to be more than just a biological act. God meant sex to be a one-flesh experience — the bonding of two people physically, emotionally, and spiritually for life. When you abuse sex it doesn't just damage your body, it damages you, and it damages your partner.

Journaling

❈ Now that you know the many foolish, dangerous consequences that come from having sex before marriage, any ideas on why these facts are ignored by our society?

_____

_____

_____

☀ What do you think is meant by this statement: *Girls have the most to lose by having sex before marriage.*

_____

_____

_____

_____

_____

☀ Look up Psalm 119:9 in a Bible version of your choice and copy it here. Replace the words "young person" or "young man" (depending on the version you choose) with your own name. Make it personal.

_____

_____

_____

_____

☀ What is today's date? _____. Check Appendix C for your *Password to Prayer.*

Quotable

"I believe kids can choose not to have sex. I tell them, 'If you're going to have sex, here's what it's going to cost you. Here's the price you're going to pay.'"–Pam Stenzel

Thursday • Lesson Four
The Warning Bell

Today's Passage

Read Proverbs 5:21-23

Proverbs Passkey

For a man's ways are in full view of the Lord, and he examines all his paths. Proverbs 5:21

Sounding the Alarm

Purity isn't just a state of body. It's truly a state of mind, as well. If we can somehow keep our minds pure, then it will be much easier to keep our bodies pure. Remember what you learned from Aristotle in Unit One: "Sow a thought, reap an act. Sow an act, reap a habit. Sow a habit, reap a character. Sow a character, reap a destiny."

God's Word tells us specifically how to think. In Philippians 4:8, Paul instructs the people. "Summing it all up, friends, I'd say you'll do best by filling your minds and meditating on things true, noble, reputable, authentic, compelling, gracious - the best, not the worst; the beautiful, not the ugly; things to praise, not things to curse."[12]

When I was a young teen, I was visiting at a friend's house. We were getting ready to go somewhere, and my friend decided we needed to use some perfume her mother had just bought. When we went into her mom's bathroom to find the perfume, I was surprised to see that her mother had a poster of Tom Selleck on the wall. (Who is Tom Selleck? He was a very good-looking celebrity back in the 80's.) I was stunned. I could never imagine my own mother putting up a poster of a movie star. That was something that my sister and I did. It wasn't something a grown woman did! I asked my friend, "What does your dad think about your mom having this poster up?"

My friend just laughed. "He can't stop her," she replied.

I can't help but think now the same things that I thought then. How could this woman put up this sexy picture of a man who is not her husband? How did it really make her husband feel? What kind of things did she think about when she looked at it? I would say, quite honestly, her thoughts were neither true nor noble.

Contrast that with this story. In the ninth grade, my friend Deanna was very happy about her history class. She got Mrs. Henegar* for her teacher, and she was everybody's favorite. Deanna was blessed to get in her class. Besides making history come to life through various books and hands-on lessons, Mrs. Henegar also showed movies in her class. One of the movies that she showed her class was an old western starring a young Robert Redford. (Who is Robert Redford? Some people think he is one of the best-looking men of all time!) The day before the class was to watch the movie together, Mrs. Henegar explained that she hoped they would enjoy the movie, but she would be taking the day off. The class would view the film with a substitute teacher.

"No way!" the class erupted. "Aw, c'mon, Mrs. Henegar! Don't take the day off! Come in and watch it with us!"

"I can't," she responded with a shake of her head. When the class continued to insist, Mrs. Henegar gave them this brief explanation.

"When I was young, I was crazy about Robert Redford. I thought he was the most handsome, perfect man that I had ever laid eyes on. After I was married, I realized that whenever I saw a movie starring Robert Redford, I still thought that. In fact, I would be thinking of him and dreaming of him instead of my husband. So I don't watch movies featuring Robert Redford anymore."

Mrs. Henegar's honesty had a profound effect on my friend and on me, too. I will never forget learning about this woman who managed to discern that a potentially serious problem for her marriage could come from a seemingly innocent thing like watching a movie. She heard the alarm going off in her head. She recognized the Holy Spirit's word of warning, so she took the necessary steps to completely avoid the temptation.

Purity isn't a line you draw in the sand. It's a life you live between your ears! Guard your thoughts, and it will pay off in every other area of your life.

Journaling

Many teens today get in trouble with their thought lives by the things they watch on TV and view on the Internet. How can you avoid these problems?

_____

_____

_____

_____

_____

_____

_____

_____

❤ What are some things you *can* think about that would be honoring to God?

_____

_____

_____

_____

_____

❤ Copy Colossians 3:2 here.

_____

_____

_____

_____

❤ Work on your passage for memorization.

❤ What is today's date? _____. Check Appendix C for your *Password to Prayer*.

Quotable

"All the great temptations appear first in the region of the mind and can be fought and conquered there. We have been given the power to close the door of the mind. We can lose this power through disuse or increase it by use, by the daily discipline of the inner man in things which seem small and by reliance upon the word of the Spirit of truth. It is God that worketh in you, both to will and to do of His good pleasure. It is as though He said, 'Learn to live in your will, not in your feelings.'" –Amy Carmichael

Friday • Lesson Five
Weekending

Today is your day to:

❀ Complete any unanswered questions from this week's lessons.

❀ Read back through Proverbs 5 and your journal entries for this week.

❀ Do some soul-searching about what God is teaching you. Record your thoughts below.

_____

_____

_____

_____

❀ Work on your Scripture memory passage. You can do it!

❀ What is today's date? _____. Check Appendix C for your *Password to Prayer.*

❀ Don't forget this week's **EXTRA!** Visit your local crisis pregnancy center. Call ahead to let them know you are coming. Take a gift of diapers, wipes, or baby formula with you.

Unit Six · Preview
Wisdom Stays Out of Trouble

Monday

Mouthy Messes: Before It Gets Cold

Tuesday

Active Ants: High Hopes for the Greatest Generation

Wednesday

Terrible Troublemakers: 7 UPs God Hates

Thursday

A Pretty Princess: The Necklace

Friday

Weekending

This Week's EXTRA!

Ask a grandparent or an older person you know what "work ethic" means. Ask him or her how the work ethic of our country has changed (or if it has). Record this person's thoughts on this week's Weekending page.

Monday • Lesson One
Mouthy Messes

Today's Passage

Read Proverbs 6:1-5

Proverbs Passkey

Go and humble yourself; press your plea with your neighbor!
Allow no sleep to your eyes, no slumber to your eyelids.
Proverbs 6:3b,4

Before It Gets Cold

Your Scripture reading for today discusses the trouble that our tongues can cause. Sometimes we say things too quickly. Sometimes we wish that we could take back things that we have said in the heat of anger or from the depths of a bad mood. Sometimes it is our inexperience that causes us to blurt out things that we later realize we shouldn't have said. In these particular verses, King Solomon is instructing his child on the best way to get out of a verbal contract.

In our American culture, the use of credit (buying something now that you will pay for later) is widely accepted. People make most major purchases by using a credit card and making payments over a period of time. In Israel, however, borrowing was something done only in the most critical circumstances. Back then and today, anytime that borrowing is done, a guarantee must be made, insuring that the borrower will pay back the lender. King Solomon told his son, "Look, don't ever say that you will pay for another person's debts! Don't get yourself into financial messes with your mouth!"

Financial messes aren't the only kinds of problems we can get ourselves into with our mouths. There are a lot of things we can say that will end up "trapping" us. I had something happen to me just recently that proves the point.

When an older gentleman ran into my van last summer, I had to deal with his insurance company in order to be compensated for the damage he had caused. The company was very slow to help me, even though their client was the sole cause of the accident.

My family had been looking forward to my son David's special birthday trip to the Superman museum in Metropolis, Illinois. He was taking along a friend, and there would have been plenty of room for everyone to travel comfortably in our van (which was totaled in the wreck). However, there was not enough room for six people in the rental car the insurance company had provided us. The insurance people were not very nice, and they were not easy to work with. I was afraid that David's birthday was going to be ruined because we weren't going to be able to make the trip without a larger vehicle.

I called the company. Since the man I needed to talk with was not available, I left a message on his voice mail. In fact, I proceeded to give him an earful as I let him have it for the terrible service we had received from the company and for single-handedly ruining my son's ninth birthday! When I was finished with my tirade, I hung up the phone.

I tried to go about my daily activities, but it wasn't very long before God began to convict me with the same words that I use on my kids. "Let's be sunshine," I like to tell them. "You never know what someone is going through, so be sunshine for other people." That insurance guy didn't need me to vent my frustration on his voice mail. Who knows what kind of life he lived? Who knows what kind of pressure he was under? Were my actions going to do anything to point him to Christ? No, I'm afraid not.

What do you do when you say things that you wish you hadn't said? King Solomon's instructions were mine that day: "Go and humble yourself; press your plea with your neighbor! Allow no sleep to your eyes, no slumber to your eyelids" (Proverbs 6:3b,4). I reached for the phone and called the man again. Once more, I was transferred to his voice mail. I left a much different message this time. I apologized for what I said and asked him to forgive me. It wasn't easy, but it would have been even harder to do if I had waited until the next day or the next week. God doesn't want us to be trapped by our words. If we find ourselves in a bind, the best thing to do is to apologize — immediately!

I received a phone call from the insurance man later that day. He said in all his years of working for that company, he had received many calls like the first message I left, but none like the second message. No one had ever apologized to him for being rude. He forgave me, and he told me that I had actually made his day!

When I was young, if I ever said something that I shouldn't, or took a "tone" with my parents, my mother would say to me, "You better take that back before it gets cold." We can talk our way into messes, but if we try hard enough, we can talk our way out of them, especially when we start with an apology. Jesus told His disciples, "Let me tell you something: Every one of these careless words is going to come back to haunt you. There will be a time of Reckoning. Words are powerful; take them seriously."[13]

Journaling

❊ Read James 3:1-12. Copy verse two here.

_____

_____

_____

❉ What do you do when you say something you wish you hadn't?

_____

_____

_____

_____

_____

❉ How do you treat people when they come to you with an apology?

_____

_____

_____

_____

_____

❉ Work on your passage for memorization.

❉ What is today's date? _____. Check Appendix C for your *Password to Prayer*.

Quotable

"Purity of attitude results in purity of word. Are you careful about the words that you speak? Are your words a blessing to others? Are your words true? Are they trustworthy? Are your words sweet to the ear? Loving words are a decision. Make the decision to speak the truth in love!" –Betty Huizenga

Tuesday • Lesson Two
Active Ants

Today's Passage

Read Proverbs 6:6-15

Proverbs Passkey

Go to the ant, you sluggard; consider its ways and be wise!
Proverbs 6:6

High Hopes for the Greatest Generation

work ethic: The attitude of a group or a society toward work, especially the attitude or belief that work is good for man and higher on society's scale of values than play or leisure.[14]

For eight years, my family lived in a wonderful house with only one problem. Ants showed up every spring. Not just one or two ants, but we had literally colonies of ants that claimed our home as theirs. When we were moving to Nashville and first went to look at this house, I noticed a few ants on the kitchen floor. At the time, I thought, *Oh, a little bug spray will get rid of those ants. No problem.* I didn't know, however, just how much of a problem they would be.

Ants are hard workers. They have no rulers, but each colony of ants has three classes: the queens, the workers, and the males. They work hard to provide food for themselves and their young. They have a strong work ethic.

Some people think that Americans have lost our *work ethic*. Americans today are not as concerned with great accomplishments as we once were. Over fifty years ago, at the conclusion of World War II, Americans came back from a hard-fought victory ready to make wonderful lives for themselves. This particular group of Americans has been labeled "The Greatest Generation" by author Tom Brokaw. In his book by that name, Brokaw writes:

> At a time in their lives when their days and nights should have been filled with innocent **adventure**, love, and the lessons of the workaday world, they were fighting in the most primitive conditions possible across the bloodied landscape of France, Belgium, Italy, Austria, and the coral islands of the Pacific. They answered the call to save the world from the two most **powerful** and ruthless military machines ever assembled, instruments of conquest in the hands of fascist maniacs. They faced great odds and a late start, but they did not protest. They succeeded on every front. They won the war; they saved the world. They came home to joyous and short-lived **celebrations** and immediately began the task of rebuilding their lives and the world they wanted. They married in record numbers and gave birth to another distinctive generation, the Baby Boomers. A **grateful** nation made it possible for more of them to attend college than any society had ever educated, anywhere. They gave the world new science, literature, art, industry and economic strength unparalleled in the long curve of history.

Perhaps these folks were the greatest generation because they saw what could happen if they didn't work hard enough. With their own eyes, they saw countries ravaged by cruel dictators because people didn't fight hard enough for freedom. Unfortunately, today's generation of young adults has known only peace and prosperity, for the most part. In exchange for living pleasant lives, we've lost our motivation to make things better. We seem to be okay with things the way they are.

The truth is that things are not okay. Our country is on the edge of collapse because the forces of evil are not being reigned in through the prayers of God's people. Have Christians forgotten God's ways?

The value of every human life is right. Abortion is wrong.

Marriage as defined by Almighty God, a commitment made between one man and one woman, is right. Homosexuality is wrong.

Loving your neighbor is right. Racism is wrong.

Maintaining a healthy lifestyle through proper nutrition and exercise is right. Drugs are wrong.

Living for Christ is right. Living for yourself is wrong.

I've got high hopes for you and for your brothers and sisters. I personally believe that yours will be the greatest generation. Are you willing to confront the culture with God's truth? Just as an ant can move things that are double and triple his own size, we can move things in our world that are seemingly immovable through the power of the God of the Universe, who bends His ear to hear our prayers.

One of the reasons the ants in our old house were so hard to get rid of was because every spring I had a new generation of ants moving in. I would get rid of one set, then, *here came their babies*! They came even more quickly because they were using the ant superhighways that their parents had built. They didn't have to do as much work because a path had already been routed for them. Rather than become lazy, however, they used the time and energy they would have spent foraging new tunnels to provide for their families and to build their colonies.

Your parents are doing everything they can to lay the groundwork for you, to build the tunnels, pave the way, and provide the best roadmap available. Don't let that make you lazy in your faith. Let it spur you on to greater heights.

Journaling

One of the favorite songs of the "greatest generation" was "High Hopes," by Sammy Cahn. Take a look at an excerpt from the lyrics:

Just what makes that little ol' ant
Think he'll move that rubber tree plant?
Anyone knows an ant can't
Move a rubber tree plant!
But he's got high hopes... he's got high hopes!
He's got high, apple pie in the sky hopes!
So any time you're getting low
'Stead of letting go,
Just remember that ant.
Oops! There goes another rubber tree plant.

❋ What is the point of the song?

_____

_____

_____

_____

❋ How is the ant going to accomplish what he wants to do?

_____

_____

_____

_____

❋ What are some things you want to do that you can accomplish with hard work?

_____

_____

✳ What are some things that can only be accomplished through prayer?

_____

_____

_____

_____

✳ Copy Matthew 19:26 here.

_____

_____

_____

_____

✳ What is today's date? _____. Check
Appendix C for your *Password to Prayer*.

Quotable

*"We need leaders who add value to the people and the
organization they lead; who work for the benefit of others
and not just for their own personal gain; who inspire and
motivate rather than intimidate and manipulate; who live with
people to know their problems and live with God in order to solve
them; and who follow a moral compass that points in the right direction regardless of
the trends." –Mary Kay Ash*

Wednesday • Lesson Three
Terrible Troublemakers

Today's Passage

Read Proverbs 6:16-19

Proverbs Passkey

There are six things the Lord hates, seven that are detestable to him: . . . Proverbs 6:16

7 "Ups" God Hates

There it is. Right there in the Word of God, Proverbs 6:16-19 lists seven things that God hates. This list deserves our serious consideration. To me, it is a very uncomfortable feeling to think that I could be doing something that God hates. I don't want that in my life! I want to be as far away from that as I can be. Let's take a look at what *not* to do.

Act UP. What the NIV translation calls "haughty eyes," other translations call *a proud look* (TEV), *arrogant eyes* (God's Word), and *eyes of pride* (the Bible in Basic English). There were some girls in my middle school who thought they were very cool—so much better than everyone else. They never said that's what they thought about themselves. They didn't have to. Their eyes told the whole story. The way they looked at other people reflected the disdain and snobbery that was in their hearts. God hates that.

Talk it UP. The second troublemaker on the list is a lying tongue. Why is it that Satan can so easily fool us into thinking that lying will solve our problems? It never, ever will. It only makes the tangle harder to get out. Lying presents us with many more problems than the one with which we began. God hates that.

Cut UP. What could be more wicked than hands that shed innocent blood? Looking at the recorded accounts of the murder of our Lord Jesus, we find Pilate, the Roman governor, as the key decision-maker in the final verdict. Pilate didn't want to crucify Jesus. He said that he couldn't find that Jesus had done anything wrong. Yet to save his political position of power, he let the people have their way and sentenced Jesus to crucifixion. Pilate's hands were guilty of shedding innocent blood, and he knew it. Matthew 27:24 tells us, "So [Pilate] sent for a bowl of water and washed his hands before the crowd, saying, 'I am innocent of the blood of this man. The responsibility is yours!'" I don't think he could get out of murder that easily, do you? God hates that.

Think UP. There really are people who sit around all day and think about doing terrible things. Their hearts are busy devising wicked things to do. Sometimes people might be motivated by what they see on TV. Sometimes people are motivated by revenge, hate, or unforgiveness. There is so much good that could be done in this world. There are many worthwhile organizations that would love to have the time and energy that some people spend inventing evil things to do. A mind is a terrible thing to waste. God hates that.

Hurry UP. It seems that some people just want to get into trouble. They are actually in a hurry to be up to no good. Their feet rush them to parties and other places where they can hurt themselves and others. God is never in a hurry; have you noticed that?

Do you remember the story of the adulterous woman? This woman was caught committing adultery, and the religious leaders of the town brought her to Jesus. They were in a hurry to punish her and to trap him. Was Jesus in a hurry? Not one bit. He stooped down to write on the ground.

He told them that the one without sin could cast the first stone at the woman. All of a sudden, no one was in a hurry. They weren't in a hurry to take an honest look at the evil in their own lives, just in a hurry to bring trouble on others. God hates that.

Make UP. It looks like God is mentioning lying twice in this passage. He is, but this second time is qualified by "lying under oath." A person who lies under oath is lying when they have promised to tell the truth, and most likely, someone else's life or reputation is at stake. God hates that.

Stir UP. You know the kind of person who likes to get things stirred up. This is a person who tells one person something, gets a reaction, and then goes and tells someone else what happened. Stirring up trouble is something godly women should stay away from, and yet, it seems that gossip is nearly irresistible. Resist it! Friendships can break, churches can split, and peaceful neighbors can become bitter enemies when someone begins to stir up trouble. God hates that.

Journaling

☀ Are you surprised by any of the things that God hates?

_____

_____

_____

_____

_____

_____

☀ Why do you think lying (although different forms of it) was mentioned twice?

_____

_____

_____

_____

_____

_____

_____

☀ What is today's date? _____. Check
Appendix C for your *Password to Prayer*.

Quotable

"Suppose someone should offer me a plateful of crumbs after I had eaten a T-bone steak. I would say, 'No, thank you. I am already satisfied.' Christian, that is the secret — you can be so filled with the things of Christ, so enamored with the things of God that you do not have time for the sinful pleasures of the world." –Billy Graham

Thursday • Lesson Four
A Pretty Princess

Today's Passage

Read Proverbs 6:20-35

Proverbs Passkey

Bind them upon your heart forever; fasten them around your neck.
Proverbs 6:21

The Necklace[15]

A beautiful princess received a rare and expensive diamond necklace from her father, the king. As he lovingly presented the gift to her, he said, "Daughter, you may think this piece of jewelry is now your most valuable possession. Indeed, its value surpasses that of almost everything your mother and I have ever given you. It is worth more than your fine clothes and the luxurious linens on your bed. It is more valuable than any of your other bracelets and rings."

The king paused as he fastened the ornate chain around the girl's slim neck. "But Daughter, there is something I have given you which I pray you have received. It is far more precious than riches. It is wisdom. Let this necklace be a reminder to you of the teachings you have learned here in the castle: *love, joy, peace, patience, kindness, goodness, faithfulness, gentleness, and self-control.* Remember, no necklace is as beautiful as the godly young woman who wears it." After many hugs, kisses, and words of thanks, the princess left to show the necklace to everyone in the kingdom.

Early the next morning, the princess went to the river for a bath. After a refreshing soak in the cool water, she dried off and began to get dressed.

But where was the necklace? The princess searched among her night things, which she had left on the bank. She searched through the tall grasses along the shore where she had put her day clothes. She searched all the way down to the rocky edge of the water, but it was nowhere to be found. In a panic, she ran crying to tell her father, who immediately sent out his men to look for the necklace. The king's men searched all day, but they could not find it. An alarm was issued alerting the entire kingdom that the necklace had vanished.

Late that afternoon, a woodcutter came to the castle. He had stopped by the river for a drink of water after a long day of hunting. As he bent his head to drink, he saw a shiny glimmer deep in the water. It was the necklace!

Immediately the king sent out his best team of divers to retrieve the necklace. They returned empty-handed. Although they could see the diamond necklace, for some reason, they could not grasp it. They were baffled by their failure. They determined to try again at daybreak.

With a heavy heart, the princess returned to the river that night. Weeping, she prayed for God to comfort her. "I'm sorry, Lord," she sobbed. "I have never lost anything so costly in my life."

Kneeling beneath a large oak tree, the princess gazed up at the clear night sky. The stars, like so many jewels, glistened with the rich glory of Heaven. Suddenly, she sensed she was not alone. The king had followed her to the river. He stood quietly behind her.

"Daughter," he whispered tenderly, "you weep over the loss of a necklace. It is not important! Don't you understand? True wealth is in the teachings of the Kingdom. You will never lose the truth of God's Word."

He joined her under the tree, wrapping a strong arm around her shoulders. "No, true wisdom can never be lost. However, you may choose to forsake Kingdom teachings. One day, you may want to abandon all you've been taught. But I pray that day never comes. I pray you decide to wear the truth constantly as a beautiful ribbon around your heart."

The princess snuggled into her father's embrace. "Oh, Daddy," she said, sniffling. "I will choose the Kingdom. I will choose Truth. Always."

The two gazed contentedly at the clear night sky, looking up through the branches of the tree. The velvety blue sky sparkled with stars. The intricate webbing of the tree looked like many chains, all studded with diamonds.

"Daddy," the princess spoke. "Do you see that star that is shining brighter than all the rest? I think I could reach out and touch it! It looks like it is actually sitting on that tree limb!"

The king leaned forward, squinting his eyes to see what his daughter saw. "Ahhh!" he said triumphantly. He stretched, reaching up for the star. Then laughing, he placed it in his daughter's hand. It was the necklace!

The princess was stunned. "What's going on?" she cried. "Daddy, how did this happen? I can't believe it!"

The king, smiling from ear to ear, explained, "Daughter, the necklace was on the tree branch all the time. You yourself must have hung it there before you bathed this morning."

Popping her hand over her mouth, the princess's eyes grew wide. She nodded her head gleefully. "I remember! Now I remember!"

The king looked over the peaceful water. "What the woodcutter and all my divers saw was merely a reflection in the river. It was not the real thing."

"Oh, Daddy!" the princess said. "That's what you've been trying to tell me all this time! This necklace is just a reflection of the teachings, isn't it?"

"Yes, Daughter," the king smiled. "Yes, now you understand."

Journaling

♥ What is the most valuable thing you own? What is the most costly item in your home? Have you ever lost something that was expensive?

_____

_____

_____

_____

♥ Write Proverbs 6:20 here. Depending on the translation you choose, change the word "son" to "daughter," or use your own name.

_____

_____

_____

_____

♥ What would it mean to "forsake" your mother's teaching? List three things your mother has taught you.

_____

_____

_____

_____

♥ What is the significance of wearing something around your neck?

_____

_____

_____

_____

_____

♥ Work on your passage for memorization.

♥ What is today's date? _____. Check Appendix C for your *Password to Prayer*.

Quotable

"Well, why do people spend so much time studying the Bible? How much do you need to know? We invest all this time in understanding the text which has a separate life of its own and we think we're being more pious and spiritual when we're doing it. But it's all to be lived. It was given to us so we could live it." –Eugene Peterson

Friday • Lesson Five
Weekending

Today is your day to:

❀ Complete any unanswered questions from this week's lessons.

❀ Read back through Proverbs 6 and your journal entries for this week.

❀ Do some soul-searching about what God is teaching you. Record your thoughts below.

_____

_____

_____

_____

❀ Work on your Scripture memory passage. You can do it!

❀ What is today's date? _____. Check Appendix C for your *Password to Prayer*.

❀ Don't forget this week's **EXTRA!** Ask a grandparent or an older person you know what "work ethic" means. Ask him or her how the work ethic of our country has changed (or if it has). Record this person's thoughts here.

_____

_____

Unit Seven • Preview
Written on Your Heart

Monday

Wisdom Recalls WWJD: An Instant Reflex

Tuesday

Wisdom Recognizes the Enemy: Taken by Surprise

Wednesday

Wisdom Retains Her Innocence: He Said, She Said

Thursday

Wisdom Rests on a Firm Foundation: Christ, the Cornerstone

Friday

Weekending

This Week's EXTRA!

Research the ordeal of missionaries Dayna Curry and Heather Mercer.
Check for information on the Internet and/or read *Prisoners of Hope:*
The Story of our Captivity and Freedom in Afghanistan by Dayna Curry
and Heather Mercer.

Monday • Lesson One
Wisdom Recalls WWJD

Today's Passage

Read Proverbs 7:1-5

Proverbs Passkey

Keep my commands and you will live; guard my teachings as the apple of your eye. Proverbs 7:2

An Instant Reflex

A few years ago when my son David was 4 years old, he asked for one of those popular WWJD bracelets. He had noticed several people at church wearing them. I thought it was a great idea. The sooner we learn to ask ourselves, "What would Jesus do?" the better!

We bought one at the Christian bookstore. I tried to explain to David, in words simple enough for a four-year-old, the concept behind WWJD. I was sure he understood because the rest of that afternoon and evening, David was an extremely good boy. He played nicely with his brother and sister and was very obedient. The next morning, however, he had barely gotten up when I heard cries coming from the living room. Danya, then 6 years old, was holding her stomach and crying, "He hit me!"

Wise Up!

I began to comfort Danya and looked at David questioningly. "What did we talk about yesterday, son?" I asked. "Did you remember to ask yourself WWJD?"

"It's okay, Momma," he said in all innocence. "I'm not wearing my bracelet today."

While it's reasonable for a 4-year-old to have that kind of limited understanding of Christianity, I have to wonder about the rest of us. What's our excuse? All too often people think they can live Christian lives that are inconsistent with the concept of Lordship. I've seen Christian bumper stickers on cars carrying drivers that don't have any road manners at all. I've seen teenagers wearing cross necklaces who are cursing a blue streak. I knew a boy who was active in his youth group but collected beer bottles and had them prominently displayed, sort of like trophies, in his bedroom. What is the deal with that? Is our Christianity just an outward display of religion? Or is Christianity a relationship that is driven to pursue an authentic submission to Jesus Christ as Lord?

Dayna Curry and Heather Mercer were serving as missionaries in Afghanistan in 2001 when they were arrested and held prisoner for witnessing to others about their faith. They were rescued after spending 105 days in captivity. When the plight of these two young women was made public by the media, reporters and columnists as well as Americans in general were sincerely bewildered. They didn't understand the whole idea of foreign missions. They could not grasp why Dayna and Heather would want to present Christianity to a culture already steeped in their own centuries-old faith. People wanted to know why two young women would risk their lives to go to a dangerous country where the people didn't want to hear what they had to say. But Heather insisted that was not true. "That's a big fat lie," she said. "All over the world there are 2.5 billion people who are waiting to hear about the love of Jesus."[16]

I believe that the world has a hard time understanding Christians because in spite of God's call to total obedience, we lead lives very much like that of non-Christians. Women like Dayna and Heather stand out because they are really living the Christian life.

I used to work with an Egyptian man named Khalil. Khalil was a devout Muslim. His co-workers respected him for his strict adherence to his beliefs. He really stood out from the crowd because he was different. He lived the Muslim life and stuck to all of the rituals that went along with it. People were very interested in his religion because he was a good representative of it. They asked him lots of questions about it because he made it look attractive. He believed in something, and people all over the world are dying for something to believe in. When I think about Khalil, I have to ask myself some hard questions. What do people think about Christianity when they look at my life? Does it look appealing to them? Are they interested in learning more?

In our nation of religious freedom comes a cry for tolerance that insists all roads lead to heaven. You may worship God, Allah, Buddha, the Goddess, the Supreme Being — whatever. After all, it's all the same thing, right? No. No, it's not the same. The difference in Christianity and every other belief in the world can be found in the fact that we aren't practicing a religion, but we are pursuing a relationship. That doesn't come about by wearing bracelets. It comes about by constantly examining the heart.

Journaling

❈ Copy John 14:15-17 here.

_____

_____

_____

_____

_____

_____

❋ Read today's quotable. Write down your thoughts and feelings about how Dayna and Heather reacted when they were taken prisoner. What do you think about the depth of their faith in God? They were able to trust in Him during the terrible ordeal they went through, rather than to become bitter and angry with Him.

_____

_____

_____

_____

❋ The Scripture passage you chose should be fully memorized now. Recite it from memory to a parent this week.

❋ What is today's date? _____. Check Appendix C for your *Password to Prayer.*

Quotable

"That's what we clung to, that's what we did while we were in prison, that's where we were able to enter God's presence and find comfort through the whole ordeal, and that kept our sanity, that we knew how to get in God's presence, how to look to His Word, how to run to Him in the situation, and how to support one another." –Dayna Curry

Tuesday • Lesson Two
Wisdom Recognizes the Enemy

Today's Passage

Read Proverbs 7:6-12

Proverbs Password:

I saw among the simple, I noticed among the young men, a youth who lacked judgment. Proverbs 7:7

Taken by Surprise

You know that when I was in school I sat behind a boy named Mark. Now I want you to know that I spent those same four years sitting in front of a boy named Steve Irving* in homeroom.

One morning, Steve was very busy "engraving" something on his wooden desk. Using a ball-point pen, he was carefully etching "Steve Irving is #1." As he showed me his handiwork before we left for classes, I could tell that Steve was proud of it. Steve was a fine athlete and a good-looking guy, not to mention easy-going and friendly. He must have thought that his modest announcement would be met with agreement by the people who would be sitting in his desk throughout the day. Not!

When we returned to homeroom the next morning, "Steve Irving is #1" had become "Steve Irving is #100."

The next day he was #1000. By the end of the week, the zeros had become so numerous that someone had inserted commas in order to make sense of it all. Steve Irving had become number one bazillion.

Poor Steve was truly astonished. He couldn't believe anyone would argue with his little declaration. He never thought he had any enemies.

Scripture clearly warns us Christians that we have an enemy. However, most people are shocked when Satan attacks.

We say things we wish we hadn't when we are tired and aggravated.

We tease our siblings in front of their friends and instantly wish we could take it back.

We laugh behind someone's back and then feel bad all day.

When we give in to Satan's prompting, we have no one to blame but ourselves. The writer of the book of James put it this way: "Don't let anyone under pressure to give in to evil say, 'God is trying to trip me up.' God is impervious to [not influenced by] evil, and puts evil in no one's way. The temptation to give in to evil comes from us and only us. We have no one to blame but the leering, seducing flare-up of our own lust."[17]

In the Scripture you read today, this is exactly what's happening. The young man has put himself in the way of temptation. He is walking around in dangerous territory. If you go through the wrong places, instead of avoiding them, then you are going to encounter evil; it will be waiting for you. You have an enemy. Will you recognize him? Or will you be taken by surprise?

God says the devil is like a roaring lion.[18] Lions are really sneaky. They laze around for up to 21 hours a day, and then in the darkest, coolest hours of the early morning, they begin to hunt. An African lion will target the weak, unsuspecting prey. Similarly, the devil will take aim at the weak, unsuspecting Christian. Remember Eve? She didn't know she had an enemy. But she did know what she had been told by God. Rather than listening to lies, she should have stood firm on the truth of God's instructions to her.

The lion's chief tactic is in the element of surprise. He stalks his prey, rushing in for the kill at rivers or water holes, where animals let down their guards. The devil is the same way. Skilled in his tactics, he has infiltrated the places we think are safe. His greatest strategy is in making us believe he does not exist.

Journaling

✳ A friend once told me that she believed Satan has a file folder for each person. In your file, he keeps a record of the best ways to trip you up. What do you think would be in your file? List some of your weakest areas. (For example, what really makes you mad? What ticks you off? What are the things that make you act un-Christianly?)

_____

_____

_____

_____

_____

_____

_____

_____

_____

_____

✳ Remembering the passage from James, you now know that the enemy is attacking you, but you alone are responsible for how you respond to these attacks. Take another look at your list, and write down some ideas for a more Christian response when these frustrating things happen. Pray for God to help you put this into action when you are next attacked!

_____

_____

_____

_____

✳ The Scripture passage you chose should be fully memorized now. Recite it from memory to a parent this week.

✳ What is today's date? _____. Check Appendix C for your *Password to Prayer*.

Quotable

"For more than 14 years I was the prey of the enemy. I thought I knew what was best for me. I wanted God only as my emergency Savior, when I was in a crisis and needed Him. And if you're like I was, the lion has you in his jaws."
–Dennis Rainey

Wednesday • Lesson Three
Wisdom Retains Her Innocence

Today's Passage

Read Proverbs 7:13-23

Proverbs Password:

All at once he followed her . . . little knowing it will cost him his life. Proverbs 7:22a,23b

He Said...She Said[19]

By Marilyn Morris

It was the last week in March, two months before graduation and the night air was cool. Kevin left the party at 11:30 and had only driven a block when he saw Jessica walking alone down the street. He stopped his car and asked if she wanted a ride home. She jumped in the car without hesitation, but they didn't go anywhere. At first they just talked. Then one thing led to another. The next thing Kevin knew they were having sex.

Kevin then drove around the corner and dropped Jessica off in front of her house and he went home . . . Or at least that's the story Kevin told the police. The story Jessica told was very different.

According to Jessica, she left the party around 11:30 and started her short walk home when Kevin

pulled up beside her and offered to take her home. The night air was cool and she took him up on the offer without hesitation. When she got in the car, she said he forced himself on her and raped her. The attorney telling the story said Kevin escaped going to prison for only one reason—his parents had the money to pay for a really good attorney. Without paying the $125,000 for a top notch attorney, Kevin might be sitting in prison today. The attorney went on to say this cat and mouse game of "He said / She said" goes on all the time.

So who was the innocent victim in this story? Was it Jessica? Did Kevin actually force her to have sex that evening? Will she be dealing with devastating memories that will haunt her for the rest of her life? Or was Kevin the innocent victim? Did Jessica make up the entire story while destroying Kevin's reputation, not to mention costing Kevin's parents over $100,000? No one but Kevin and Jessica will ever know the truth about what transpired that night because there were no other witnesses.

Now consider the pending case against Kobe Bryant. Kobe was on top of the world. In 1996 he went from playing basketball in high school directly into the pros and had an impressive rookie season with the LA Lakers. The following year he became the youngest All-Star in NBA history. His wholesome image as an athlete, husband, and father provided multimillion-dollar endorsements. It was as if nothing could bring Kobe Bryant down. That is until June 30th when he opened the door and invited a 19-year-old girl into his hotel room in Colorado. A few hours later the cat and mouse game of "He Said / She Said" was set into motion and Kobe Bryant's life changed forever.

Kobe has now been charged with sexually assaulting the 19-year-old girl. If he is convicted, it is possible Kobe could spend the rest of his life in prison.

Kobe and Kevin seem to have a great deal in common. Both are in the prime of their lives. Kobe is 25. Kevin is 18. No doubt both felt somewhat invincible. Kobe was looking forward to yet another successful year with the NBA making millions of dollars while Kevin was looking forward to graduation and then heading off to college. Both men have been charged with rape. And while we may never know if Kobe and Kevin are innocent or guilty, we do know one thing for certain about both of these two young men. Had they chosen sexual abstinence until marriage and faithfulness inside marriage [Kobe is a husband and father], neither would have gone through the nightmare and public humiliation they now face.

Abstinence would have provided 100 percent protection for Kobe and Kevin as well as 100 percent protection for their families. Kobe would simply be known as one of America's top basketball superstars, and Kevin would be just another cute freshman guy on a college campus. But now because of one brief moment in history, people will always remember them as two more guys who have been accused of rape.

Journaling

☀ Eventually Jessica dropped the charges against Kevin. What do you think would make a person lie the way she did? Think about it, and list several reasons.

_____

_____

_____

_____

_____

_____

_____

_____

_____

_____

☀ As of the time of publication of *Wise Up!*, no one knows what is going to happen with Kobe Bryant's case. He has admitted to committing adultery, but he says he did not rape the woman. In other words, she was a willing partner, and he didn't force her to have sex. Regardless of the outcome of the trial, what kind of impact do you think this event will have on his marriage, his future, and his basketball career?

_____

_____

_____

_____

_____

☀ The Scripture passage you chose should be fully memorized now. Recite it from memory to a parent this week.

☀ What is today's date? _____. Check Appendix C for your *Password to Prayer*.

Quotable

"Sure, you can learn from making mistakes. But the emphasis in Scripture is on being obedient to God in the first place. Proverbs tells us to listen to what wisdom has to say, listen to the pain that you can avoid if you do the right thing." –Joshua Harris

Thursday • Lesson Four
Wisdom Rests on a Firm Foundation

Today's Passage

Read Proverbs 7:24-27

Proverbs Passkey

Many are the victims she has brought down; her slain are a mighty throng. Her house is a highway to the grave, leading down to the chambers of death. Proverbs 7:26,27

Christ, the Cornerstone

Faith•quake: (fAth′kwAk) **n.** a shaking or trembling of one's faith caused by extreme tragedy or disaster and producing an upheaval which leads to radical change

In July, 1986, Doug and Evon Herman were in love with each other and with the Lord. The young couple were the proud parents of their toddler son, Joshua Ryan. Doug was pursuing a degree from a Bible college while employed as a full-time youth pastor. Sweethearts since their high school days and married just after Evon graduated, the Hermans were eagerly serving the Lord together in ministry. Bright, energetic, and upbeat, they looked forward to passing on their heritage of faith to a family they hoped would include several more children.

Their hopes were destroyed when Evon's gynecologist summoned the young family to his office. Eighteen months earlier, just after delivering Josh, Evon had required a blood transfusion. The doctor informed them that one of the two units of blood given to Evon at that time had been infected with the HIV virus (the virus that causes AIDS). The Hermans' young lives were devastated as the doctor explained that now tests showed that Evon was infected with HIV as well. (See Journaling for a definition of AIDS.)

Doug, who grew up in a Christian home, explains, "I had learned that if you serve God and if you live right, He will bless you. If you serve God and if you live right, He will protect you. But that was not what was happening in my life."

Many times, Christians believe that if they do everything right, God will keep His hand of blessing on them. "The reality is that it might not happen," states Doug. "When tragedy occurs—when somebody's spouse leaves them, when an earthquake or a disaster falls, when we lose loved ones, or when we lose our physical ability because of cancer or Crohn's disease, we think 'God, where are you? What did You do?' Our faith is so tied to our temporal, physical experiences that we can't get past those faithquake experiences to find out that our faith still is intact, regardless of what happens."

After going through the tragedy of losing his wife and also a baby daughter, Doug readily admits that there is a difference in where he is now, spiritually, and where his faith was during those trials. "My faith today is not based on what God does or does not do for me. Whether God gives me all the blessings of the world or if my life is full of tragedies, my faith must be based on Who He is. He's still my God, and I'll serve Him regardless. Before, my faith was based in the promises, not in the One Who makes the promises."

Doug went from one spiritual point to the other by asking God the difficult questions that were coursing through his mind and heart. "If you're going to question God," he advises, "then don't stop until you find an answer. Start digging—but don't stop until you hit something solid, like the cornerstone of your faith: Christ."

As Doug turned to his Bible for answers, he found a camaraderie with several heroes of the faith who had faithquakes of their own. One was John the Baptist.

John the Baptist was Jesus' blood relative. He knew Christ. Yet John found himself in a dungeon, about to be killed by the wicked Herod, even though he knew he had done nothing to deserve such a punishment. John knew Jesus was God, but Christ was not doing what John thought He would do. Confused, John sent two of his disciples to ask Jesus if He was indeed the Messiah or if they should be looking for someone else.

Doug explains, "Jesus sent word to John assuring him that yes, He was the Messiah. Jesus also told the messengers to tell John, basically, 'Blessed is he who does not stumble on account of me. Blessed is he whose faith does not falter, who doesn't go through a faithquake because I'm not doing what he wants Me to do.'[20]

"You have to realize that God will do what He wants to do. We must still trust Him, even when things fall apart—even if we're about to get beheaded! If we continue to believe in Him and trust Him, then we are highly blessed."

God wants you to know Him. He wants you to rely on Him and trust in Him, resting on the foundation of Christ as the cornerstone of your life. Trust Him through the good times and the bad times. You will be highly blessed.

Journaling

♥ AIDS stands for Acquired Immunodeficiency Syndrome. This disease renders the body unable to fight off the many infectious diseases it normally could if it were healthy. When the first cases of the disease were reported back in the 1980's, doctors and other healthcare workers didn't understand how it was spread. (Now we know that AIDS is spread mostly through sexual contact.) Unfortunately, the HIV virus contaminated much of the nation's blood supply before anyone knew the damage it could cause. Our blood supply is safe today because all donated blood is tested for AIDS. Evon Herman was a victim of AIDS due to circumstances that were far beyond her control. What is the number one thing you can do to avoid the HIV virus?

_____

_____

_____

_____

♥ Have you experienced tragedy in your life? How can God use difficult times to draw us close to Him?

_____

_____

_____

_____

_____

_____

_____

♥ Are you ever tempted to think that if you are a good person, God owes you something? Do you get upset when things go well for a person who is not godly? Look up Matthew 5:45. What is Jesus saying?

_____

_____

_____

_____

_____

♥ The Scripture passage you chose should be fully memorized now. Recite it from memory to a parent this week.

♥ What is today's date? _____. Check Appendix C for your *Password to Prayer*.

Quotable

"We presume that it's our right to have health. It's our right to be successful. It's our right, because we are children of the King, to have victory, including physical well-being, a lack of pain, and a lack of suffering. [But] faith in God and becoming a child of the King means that we have citizenship in His Kingdom. It doesn't mean that our lives are going to be perfect." –Doug Herman

Friday • Lesson Five
Weekending

Today is your day to:

❀ Complete any unanswered questions from this week's lessons.

❀ Read back through Proverbs 7 and your journal entries for this week.

❀ Do some soul-searching about what God is teaching you. Record your thoughts below.

_____

_____

_____

_____

❀ Choose another Scripture passage to begin working on. Write the reference here: _____. Try to complete it by the end of this study. Scripture memory should be an ongoing part of your life!

❀ Check Appendix C for your *Password to Prayer*.

❀ Don't forget this week's **EXTRA!** Research the ordeal of missionaries Dayna Curry and Heather Mercer. Check for information on the Internet and/or read *Prisoners of Hope: The Story of our Captivity and Freedom in Afghanistan* by Dayna Curry and Heather Mercer.

Unit Eight · Preview
Wisdom's Invitation

Monday

Where: A Busy Intersection

Tuesday

When: A Daily Date

Wednesday

Who: King Solomon and You

Thursday

RSVP: The Courtesy of a Reply is Requested

Friday

Weekending

This Week's EXTRA!

Read the book of Ecclesiastes in a modern version. (You have this week and next to complete this EXTRA!)

Monday • Lesson One
Where?

Today's Passage

Read Proverbs 8:1-11

Proverbs Passkey

Choose my instruction instead of silver, knowledge rather than choice gold, for wisdom is more precious than rubies, and nothing you desire can compare with her. Proverbs 8:10,11

A Busy Intersection

The entire book of Proverbs is an invitation—a cry—beckoning the reader to come to wisdom. In fact, Eugene Peterson, author of the paraphrase "The Message," translates Solomon's words in this way: ***Wisdom cries out from the busiest intersection in town.***

When I visited New York City, I saw firsthand the busiest intersection in the country: Times Square. I had never seen anything like it in my life. They call New York "the city that never sleeps" because the lights never go out on Times Square. You can walk outside anytime of the night, and Times Square is as bright as day because of all the lights—the streetlights, the brilliant glow from the posh hotels, the lights from the zillions of billboards and ads that are all over the place, and even the beams from the headlights of the cars and taxis that creep along the crowded streets.

Times Square is noisy. Horns are honking constantly. Vendors market their wares with loud voices. Music blares from shops longing to lure customers in to view their merchandise. Television networks have huge screens facing the square, with perfectly lipsticked talking heads proclaiming the latest news, sports scores, and stock market numbers. And the people! The people have a sound all their own. Their feet are clomping, clipping, and clanking down the sidewalk. Humans of all languages—all colors, shapes, and sizes—collide on these streets where the world crosses paths. It's Times Square, the busiest intersection in town.

My husband and I, along with two friends, rode through these streets in a genuine New York City taxi. I braced myself for an exciting ride. I had heard all about the crazy cab drivers! Our driver competently raced down the street, whipping in and out between cars and back and forth between lanes. Then, quite unexpectedly, he slammed on his brakes. Up ahead, I could make out the shadowy figure of a man waving his arms, imploring us to stop. He was standing in the middle of the road, just as we were approaching Times Square.

Frankly, I was a bit scared. After all, I've seen enough TV shows to know New York City is dangerous. At first, I thought for certain that we were going to hit the man. Then, I considered that the guy could be flagging us down in order to rob us or carjack the cab! All sorts of crazy scenarios raced through my mind.

As our flustered cabbie came to a screeching halt just inches from this young man, the guy began to sing. Yes, he sang! Taking advantage of the cab's headlights as though he were under the spotlight in a Broadway play, he began to perform. He stood in front of a taxi full of heart-pounding, breathless, frightened tourists, and he sang at the top of his lungs, "I LOVE NEW YORK!" Obviously drunk, the young man finished his concert with a grand flourish, bowed deeply for his captive audience, and our driver put the taxi in gear and sped around him.

This guy certainly got our attention. And what was his message? He loves New York. Big deal. This drunk punk stood in front of a racing cab to deliver a worthless message. He put his life, as well as the lives of the people in my cab, in jeopardy to declare his love for a city—a love that manifested itself in getting drunk, partying, and acting stupidly.

Did I care that he loved New York? No. He didn't really love the city's lives; he merely loved the city life. Big difference.

Was his message important? No, not at all.

What does his love for New York mean to me? Nothing.

Does it make a difference in my life? Absolutely not.

But what if this had been his message:

> You - I'm talking to all of you, everyone out here on the streets . . . Don't miss a word of this - I'm telling you how to live well, I'm telling you how to live at your best . . . **Prefer my life-disciplines over chasing after money, and God-knowledge over a lucrative career. For Wisdom is better than all the trappings of wealth; nothing you could wish for holds a candle to her.**[21]

Now, there's a message worth laying down one's life for. It's important. That message needs to stop traffic! It's God's message to all people.

Journaling

❋ Draw a picture of Lady Wisdom standing in the middle of a busy intersection, proclaiming the truth of God's Word. What would this look like to you? Spend some time on this. You're the only person who ever has to see it. Think about it. Draw your masterpiece below.

❋ Why is it so difficult for the voice of wisdom to be heard at a busy intersection?

_____

_____

_____

_____

❋ What are some foolish things that cry out for your attention? How can you quiet those cries in order to listen for Wisdom's Invitation?

_____

_____

_____

_____

_____

❋ Work on your passage for memorization.

❋ What is today's date? _____. Check Appendix C for your *Password to Prayer*.

Quotable

"Choices. You make them every day. Some are small and insignificant. Others will have a profound impact on the rest of your life. The bottom line is this: the choices you make today can lead to success or serious regrets." –Marilyn Morris

Tuesday · Lesson Two
When?

Today's Passage

Read Proverbs 8:12-21

Proverbs Passkey

I love those who love me, and those who seek me find me.
Proverbs 8:17

A Daily Date

My friend Lynnae and her husband Rob had been sleeping soundly one night when they were suddenly awakened by the sound of something banging. *Thump! Thump! Thump!* Drowsily, Lynnae looked around the dark bedroom. Immediately, she noticed the lights on her clock radio were not on. "Oh," Lynnae thought, as she began to put the pieces together. "*It must be storming. The electricity has gone out. That thumping sound is the door of the shed in the backyard. It never stays closed! Rob should fix that. It bangs with the wind every time there's a storm…*" With everything settled in her mind, Lynnae began to drift back to sleep.

Suddenly, she heard the loud voice of a man yelling, "LET ME IN! LET ME IN!" Her eyes were wide open as she sat up in bed and fear gripped her heart. She could make out the shadowy image of Rob standing beside the window.

"They've cut off the power," he said. "Call the police — NOW!" From the bedroom window, Rob saw that someone had tampered with their utility box. He realized the thumping sound was a person banging on the back door, trying to break into their home. With no weapon of any kind in the house, Rob dashed to the back door, determined to somehow protect his wife and property.

"They? Who are they?" Lynnae wanted to scream as she searched frantically to find the cell phone in the dark house. Finally, she located it and was able to place a call to 911. Meanwhile, Rob began pounding on his side of the back door, screaming at the potential attacker on the other side. He got as violent and as loud as he could from his side of the door until the police arrived a few minutes later and the would-be thief ran off.

A few days later, Lynnae said, "I never went to sleep that night thinking our home would be attacked. We live in a safe neighborhood. We have close neighbors on all sides. We even live across the street from our church, where a security guard is on duty every night."

In the Bible, God warns us that our enemy, Satan, is like a thief. He attacks us when we least expect it. Does a thief call and warn you that he is going to rob you? Of course not. Likewise, Satan doesn't call ahead and say, "Hey — I'm going to tempt you at four o'clock today. Be ready."

But our Lord has told us that we *will* be tempted. We would be wise to be prepared for it. How do you prepare?

Preparation is a daily thing. Just as you get up and get dressed every day, you must wake up your spirit and get it dressed as well. Having a daily quiet time, a daily date with God, is essential to being prepared for whatever the day brings. There is, however, a problem: Because your daily date is the point at which your faith is strengthened, and it's where you learn to truly know and love God, it's the area where Satan will do his best to trip you up. If he can keep you from meeting with God, he can keep you from the benefits of God's love and wisdom in your life.

The best way to prepare for those unexpected attacks is to establish a battle plan. Meet with God every day. Read your Bible. Pray. Write in a journal. Or just sit still and think about Him. Take a few minutes each morning to tell the Lord you love Him. Thank Him for salvation. Thank Him for how wonderful it is to be growing up. Celebrate the Lord's favor and His hand of love on your life!

When Lynnae and Rob went to bed the night following the attack, things were different. This time, they were prepared for the unexpected. Each of them had a flashlight and a cell phone on their bedside tables. Outside, their utility box had been repaired and fitted with a padlock, and underneath their bed was a new gun, licensed and loaded.

Because they were prepared, they slept soundly. Nothing happened that night, or the next, or the next. But two weeks later, the same guy, the thief, returned. He pounded on the back door, screaming his head off. "LET ME IN!" he thundered. "LET ME IN!"

Lynnae immediately snatched her cell phone off the night table and dialed 911. Rob grabbed the new gun and ran toward the back door. Through the door, Rob screamed back at him, "What is your name? Who are you?"

"My name is Nathan!"

"I don't know you!" Rob cried, cocking the gun. At once, the thief ran off. He was just a bully! He had no weapons that could be used against my friends. He made a lot of noise and caused a lot of fear—but in the end, he ran away. Your enemy will run away, too, when you live a life that is daily prepared for his unexpected attacks.

Journaling

✻ Write down three reasons for having a daily date with God.

_____

_____

_____

✳ Why do you think Rob wanted to know the man's name?

_____

_____

_____

_____

✳ As Christians, when we get comfortable spiritually, we are prone to attack. What kinds of things are going on in your life when the enemy is most likely to attack you?

_____

_____

_____

_____

✳ Work on your passage for memorization.

✳ What is today's date? _____. Check Appendix C for your *Password to Prayer*.

Quotable

"Well, for me, writing in my journal and singing songs to God are my two most effective ways to communicate with God. I almost don't have a relationship with God if don't journal and I don't sing. They're my life force of relationship with God." –Lamont Hiebert (of the band Ten Shekel Shirt)

Wednesday • Lesson Three
Who?

Today's Passage

Read Proverbs 8:22-29

Proverbs Passkey

I was appointed from eternity, from the beginning, before the world began. Proverbs 8:23

King Solomon and You

By Billy Graham[22]

King Solomon, whom we think wrote Ecclesiastes, was one of the richest men who ever lived. He was also very wise. The Bible says that "Solomon's wisdom was greater than the wisdom of all the men of the East, and greater than all the wisdom of Egypt."[23] But he was searching. And his search led him everywhere. Solomon had everything one could dream of, but at the end of his search, he said, "It's worthless. Everything is vanity."[24]

Solomon gave himself to pleasure. He tried alcohol, women, music. He had 700 wives. He had 300 concubines, or mistresses. He ate the best food. He drank the finest wines. Just about everything that you're working for and dreaming about or thinking about, he had it. Solomon said, "I denied myself nothing my eyes desired; I refused my heart no pleasure."[25] He gained all the pleasure that he could find. But one day he said,

"Everything is meaningless. I'm chasing after the wind. It's vanity."[26] A person can have all the riches in the world and it won't fill the emptiness of his heart.

Think of Jesus. He had it all. But He gave His life on the cross so that you and I might live. He died on that cross. They lacerated His back. They pulled His beard. They pulled His hair. They spit on Him. Then the Roman soldiers nailed Him on a cross. They put a spike through His legs. And He hung there, bleeding, suffering. They said, "Come down from the cross, if you are the Son of God!"[27] He could have come down and swept them all into an eternity without Him, and the whole world would've been lost. But He stayed there. He knew that He was dying for you and for me. He loved you and He died for you.

When I tell you that you can put your faith in Jesus Christ and have your life changed and that you can go to heaven, it's foolish. You laugh and think, "It can't be — that somebody could die on a cross 2,000 years ago and that it would affect me today." But the Scripture says that in Jesus Christ "are hidden all the treasures of wisdom and knowledge."[28] Think of it. In Him is all knowledge. Solomon was looking for that.

When I was in high school, about 16 years of age, I went to church faithfully because my parents made me. I didn't understand very much of what I heard, but I knew that it was the thing to do. I was baptized and confirmed. But nothing brought peace to my heart. One day, an evangelist came to our town. I was against him from the start — I didn't like anything that I read or heard about him. He was there for about a month. During this time, one of the men who worked on my father's dairy farm said, "I've been going to hear this man preach in town. How about going with me?" So one night I went with him.

The evangelist didn't talk about the latest book he had read or the latest movie he had seen — he just spoke from the Bible. When he asked people to come forward to receive Christ, I went. And while I was standing there, I thought, "I'm making a fool of myself." I saw two or three of my school buddies, and they probably were snickering, but I stayed. I received Christ into my heart.

I went home that night, and I remember it was a full moon. From my bedroom window, I looked out at that moon and I thought for a long time. And then I got on my knees and I said, "O God, I don't understand all that happened tonight, but I know something good has happened to me."

And from then on, I felt different. I still made many mistakes and I still committed many sins, but I knew that Jesus was in my heart and I knew that He was taking care of all those things.

In talking about Himself, Jesus said, "One greater than Solomon is here."[29] In 1934, I made the decision to follow Christ. And I've never changed my mind. Though I have failed God many times, He has never failed me.

Solomon, too, finally came to a conclusion about how to have peace, fulfillment and a life purpose: "Fear God and keep his commandments, for this is the whole duty of man. For God will bring every deed into judgment, including every hidden thing, whether it is good or evil.[30]

Journaling

✺ Have you made a decision for Christ? In a couple of paragraphs, write down the story of the day you accepted Christ. In what ways has it affected your life? What was your life like before this decision? What is your life like now? In what ways do you want your life to serve Christ?

_____

_____

_____

_____

_____

_____

_____

_____

_____

_____

_____

_____

☀ Perhaps you've never made Jesus the Lord of your life. Have you ever prayed and asked Christ to forgive you of your sins? Have you ever truly answered the invitation He has offered you? I invite you to pray this prayer, and commit your life to Him today. He has a wonderful plan for you. Just pray: *Dear God, I am a sinner. I've done lots of wrong things in my life. I need a Savior. I need Your Son, Jesus. I want Him to be the Lord of my life. I accept the forgiveness His death bought for me, and I commit today to follow Him with my whole heart. In Jesus' Name, Amen.* If you pray this prayer for the first time today, sign and date the line below, and share the wonderful news with your parents!

_____

☀ Work on your new passage for memorization.

☀ What is today's date? _____. Check Appendix C for your *Password to Prayer*.

Quotable

"In 1934, I made the decision to follow Christ. And I've never changed my mind. Though I have failed God many times, He has never failed me." –Billy Graham

Thursday • Lesson Four
R.S.V.P.

Today's Passage

Read Proverbs 8:30-36

Proverbs Passkey

Blessed is the man [woman] who listens to me, watching daily at my doors, waiting at my doorway. Proverbs 8:34

The Courtesy of a Reply is Requested

Have you noticed that life is full of invitations? You have received lots of invitations. From the time you were a baby, you were invited to friends' homes, to your grandparents' house, and to church. As you got older, you received invitations to birthday parties, the circus, and the movies. Invitations can be divided into three groups:

Invitations that Refresh. I'm waiting for someone to invite me for a weekend at a spa. That would be refreshing! But really, anytime you are invited somewhere that makes you feel comfortable, it's refreshing. For instance, you may be invited to spend the night at a friend's house. While you are there, you and your friend spend time doing the things you love to do. You giggle, you eat your favorite foods, you watch your favorite movies and TV shows, and you sleep late the next day. It's an invitation to fun! One of my favorite things to do is enjoy an evening with friends, talking, laughing, and sharing with one another.

Invitations that Stretch. Have you ever taken a rubber band and STRETCHED it? I've received invitations that made me feel that way, stretched out of my comfort zone. My husband Rich invited me to my first minor league ballgame when we were dating. (This was long before I had children and turned into a baseball mom.) I had never been so bored in my life. I amused myself by trying out all the offerings at the concession stand. One inning I had popcorn, then a hotdog, then nachos. Finally, at the end of the seventh inning, everyone stood up. I thought we were ready to leave—but it was only the "seventh inning stretch!" I had two more innings to go, and a stomach too full to eat anything else. I was stretched to the max.

Invitations that disappoint. Maybe you've been invited to a party and the hostess ignored you the entire time you were there. Or perhaps you've been invited to a church where no one welcomed you. When things don't go the way we expect them to, we are often disappointed. I was once invited out on a date, but the young man who asked me out never came to pick me up that evening. I got "stood up." He didn't call or anything to let me know what had happened. I was very disappointed, and to be quite honest, I was angry, too! His invitation was most disappointing because it had not been sincere. It was issued with the intent to hurt.

The interesting thing about invitations is that they all come with an R.S.V.P. — the American abbreviation for the French phrase, "répondez s'il vous plaît." The English translation is: *The courtesy of a reply is requested.* In other words, what are you going to do with the invitation you have received? Will you accept the invitation or will you reject it?

Take a look at the picture you drew Tuesday. At every point of decision in your life, wisdom will be as obvious as a beautiful woman standing in the middle of a busy intersection, waving her arms and screaming for you to accept her invitation. Does she look out of place in the picture you drew? Wisdom doesn't exactly fit in with the American landscape of a bustling, chaotic city. But you notice her, don't you? You can't help it. The question is, when people who are so busy and moving so quickly through this life meet up with Wisdom, are they going to slow down? Are they going to stop and listen to Wisdom's invitation? And what will you do, sweet young lady, when you stand at a crossroads of your own? You may find yourself at one of life's intersections even today. Every intersection is an invitation to making wise choices. So, R.S.V.P.!

When someone offers you a cigarette or a beer, Wisdom will be there. When someone tells you, "One time won't hurt anything," you will hear Wisdom's voice. Wisdom's cry will rise above all the street noise: the hum of the crowd, the whiz of the vehicles, the beeping horns, and the music blaring from radios and storefronts. In reality, it is the still, small voice of a loving Father who knows what is best for you. If Jesus Christ is alive in you, that still small voice will be as vivid as a beautiful woman standing on top of a yellow taxi, waving her arms in the middle of Times Square.

Wisdom's invitation will take you to a place of deep refreshment. Will it stretch you? Absolutely. Will it disappoint you? Never. After studying Proverbs 8 this week, you have received Wisdom's invitation. Now, the courtesy of a reply is requested.

Journaling

♥ Copy this sentence: Every intersection is an invitation to making wise choices.

_____

_____

♥ Have you ever received an invitation that ended up being disappointing? What happened?

_____

_____

_____

_____

_____

_____

_____

💗 How is Wisdom's invitation different? In what specific ways will it refresh and stretch you? List three.

_____

_____

_____

_____

_____

💗 Work on your new passage for memorization.

💗 What is today's date? _____. Check Appendix C for your *Password to Prayer*.

Quotable

"The ultimate measure of a man is not where he stands in moments of comfort and convenience, but where he stands at times of challenge and controversy." –Martin Luther King Jr.

Friday • Lesson Five
Weekending

Today is your day to:

❀ Complete any unanswered questions from this week's lessons.

❀ Read back through Proverbs 8 and your journal entries for this week.

❀ Do some soul-searching about what God is teaching you. Record your thoughts below.

_____

_____

_____

_____

_____

_____

❀ Copy the Scripture you plan to memorize on a separate sheet of paper. Keep it in this notebook.

❀ What is today's date? _____. Check Appendix C for your *Password to Prayer.*

❀ Don't forget this week's **EXTRA!** Make time this week and next week to read through the book of Ecclesiastes in a Bible translation or paraphrase of your choice.

Unit Nine • Preview
Wisdom Sets a Table

Monday

The Menu: A Myriad of Choices

Tuesday

The House Specialty: A Teachable Spirit

Wednesday

The Main Course: Cleaning Your Plate

Thursday

Old Mother Hubbard: Secrets of the Cupboard

Friday

Weekending

This Week's EXTRA!

Complete your reading of Ecclesiastes.

Monday • Lesson One
The Menu

Today's Passage

Read Proverbs 9:1-6

Proverbs Passkey

Wisdom has built her house; she has hewn out its seven pillars. Proverbs 9:1

A Myriad of Choices

When I was growing up, we had church-wide fellowship meals quite often. I looked forward to those times when our church family ate together. It was so much fun! Since I grew up without any grandparents, aunts, uncles, or cousins living close by, these experiences were like a large family gathering.

The meals were never catered by a restaurant. Instead, the ladies of the church always cooked their favorite dishes and brought them to our fellowship hall in the basement of the church. The delicious aromas wafted upstairs during the worship service. I wriggled and fidgeted in my hard pew seat until I'm sure my mother thought she would have to sit on me to keep me still. As soon as the last *amen* was said, I raced from the sanctuary to the basement. Somehow I always managed to maneuver my way through the crowd and make it to the front of the line. That's so funny to me, when I look back on it, because I was such a picky eater. I don't know what I was expecting to find.

I can remember standing at the head of what seemed like an endless table spread before me, covered in crisp white tablecloths and piled high with huge amounts of food. I traipsed through the line, eyeballing the typical Southern fare: dressed eggs, baked beans, green beans, gelatin salads, cole slaw, and mashed potatoes. People would always laugh upon seeing my plate when I made it to the end of that smorgasbord. From a table heaped with choices, I took a roll and a chicken leg. And that's it.

The Bible tells the story of a young man who also stood at the head of a banquet table heaped high with food. Daniel was a young Jew who was taken into captivity when Babylon attacked Jerusalem. The Babylonian king at that time, Nebuchadnezzar, was quite a military strategist. Besides taking down the king and looting the temple of God, Nebuchadnezzar took his line of attack one step further. He sent the head of his staff, Ashpenaz, to take as war prisoners the best and the brightest young men from the best and the brightest families. These boys would become an integral part of Babylon's future.

"Select only strong, healthy, and good-looking young men," [Nebuchadnezzar] said. "Make sure they are well versed in every branch of learning, are gifted with knowledge and good sense, and have the poise needed to serve in the royal palace. Teach these young men the language and literature of the Babylonians."[31] If the king could successfully immerse these young Hebrew men into the Babylonian culture, their language and their literature, he could make them Babylonians.

As a college student, I studied French. I was never very good at actually speaking the language, but I was a decent translator when it came to reading and writing it. Before my final exam, I spent the entire day at the library, studying every chapter in my book. I wrote down every vocabulary word, re-did the exercises, and read until my eyes were bloodshot. Walking home from the library that day, I realized that I was *thinking* in French. It was a great moment! I was so into it, so totally absorbed by my review, that my brain was translating my thoughts into French, automatically! It didn't last. I made an "A" on my test, but today, nearly twenty years later, I remember only a handful of French words and a few phrases. I am not a Frenchman! I am an English-speaking American.

King Nebuchadnezzar had a good plan:

- Saturate the boys with the Babylonian culture.

- Develop loyalty and pride in these future patriots by telling them about the history of this great country.

- School them in the religion of many gods, mysticism, and superstition.

- Make them Babylonians!

The plan may have worked with some, but the plan did not work with Daniel. Daniel's soul was saturated not only with the culture of Israel—its history, its heroes, and its homelands—but Daniel's heart belonged to Israel's God. He would never be a Babylonian, no matter what he read, what he was taught, or what language he was forced to speak. More on Daniel tomorrow.

Journaling

❀ Look up Daniel 1 in your Bible. Why do you think the king wanted boys who were handsome? What difference did it make what they looked like?

_____

_____

_____

_____

_____

_____

✻ How would it feel to be taken out of your homeland and forced to live in another, adopting foreign traditions and languages?

_____

_____

_____

_____

_____

✻ What are some ways the enemy tries to immerse Christians in a worldly culture?

_____

_____

_____

_____

_____

✻ Work on your passage for memorization.

✻ What is today's date? _____. Check Appendix C for your *Password to Prayer*.

Quotable

"Rather than continue our mindless, unconscious habits, we need to be intentional and rational about what we choose to put into our bodies. We need to take a cold, hard look at the bad habits into which we have fallen and choose to make a change when we find ourselves in error." –Dr. Don Colbert, M.D.

Tuesday • Lesson Two
The House Specialty

Today's Passage
Read Proverbs 9:7-9

Proverbs Passkey

Instruct a wise man and he will be wiser still; teach a righteous man and he will add to his learning. Proverbs 9:9

A Teachable Spirit

The Israelites followed a strict diet, one that had been set up by the Lord Himself. There were certain foods they weren't allowed to eat, such as pork and lobster, but they did eat lots of fish, fruits, and vegetables. A Babylonian table and the foreign food on it would have immediately caused all kinds of *buzzers* to go off in Daniel's heart. Some Bible scholars believe that King Nebuchadnezzar's table was filled with food that had been offered to Babylonian gods. If Daniel ate it, he would be aligning himself with those who worshiped these false gods. He could not do that. He would not do that.

Daniel came up with an alternate plan which he presented to the steward, the head of the palace staff. God caused this man's heart to show favor to Daniel.

Although he initially resisted Daniel's idea for fear he would lose his job, he was persuaded to provide Daniel and his three friends with vegetables and water for a ten-day trial period. He took a chance. He allowed these boys to try something new. He was willing to see what would happen. At the end of the ten days, as you remember, Daniel and his friends were noticeably healthier and stronger than the other young men. (Don't let the fact escape you here that of the many Hebrews seized by Babylon, only these four were adhering to the strict dietary code they had all been raised on.)

The steward continued to bring Daniel the vegetables and water he requested. Notice the steward's teachable spirit. He was willing to acknowledge that Daniel's diet was obviously superior to the king's food. He freely admitted that Daniel was right.

You will never get to the point where you know everything. There will always be someone you haven't met, some place you've never been, some food you've never tasted, some tune you've never heard. While Solomon tells us in Ecclesiastes that "there is nothing new under the sun,"[32] this fact remains: Because there is so very much that is and has always been, so much to learn about, we could never know it all. This is especially true when it comes to the Word of God.

My friend Tina* was going through a difficult time in her life. She was carrying the heavy burdens of a troubled marriage, an aging mother, and her own medical problems as well. She admitted to me that she found no comfort in the Bible. Why not? Because she wasn't picking it up and reading it.

"I know what the Bible says," Tina remarked, shrugging her shoulders. "I know what's in there; I've read it enough. I don't have to keep going to it when I know what it says." Tina was dealing with a spirit of pride. Her attitude was that God couldn't teach her anything else. He couldn't offer her any hope or comfort because she already knew all He had to say.

Tina's marriage ended in divorce. Her mother passed away. Tina's personal health problems continued to escalate, resulting in several surgeries and hospitalizations. After struggling on her own for several years, she decided it was time to see what God had to say. Tina enrolled in a Bible study. God opened up His Word to her like never before. She began to read the Bible with fresh eyes and a teachable spirit. She will quickly admit to you today that even after years of studying the Scriptures, she is always learning something new.

Having a teachable spirit is simply realizing that there is always more to learn. The very best teachers are the ones who continue taking classes themselves. They continue to study, read, and learn. The very best students are the ones who understand the process of learning, which can be summed up in three words: Learning never ends. We can stop being teachable, however, when we refuse to submit to authority and decide we know it all. Even in the middle of our pride, however, God will still use people and circumstances to turn us away from what we think we know and turn us toward His Son, Jesus Christ, who is the only source of truth and wisdom.

Journaling

❋ How do you develop a teachable spirit? What can you do to become more teachable?

_____

_____

_____

_____

_____

_____

_____

❋ I overheard this conversation in the church hallway after Sunday school:

"I am learning so much from you," the young man said to his teacher, who was many years older.

"And I am learning so much from you," the teacher replied.

How could the older, wiser teacher say something like that to his student? What happens to the person who refuses to learn?

_____

_____

_____

_____

❋ Work on your passage for memorization.

❋ What is today's date? _____. Check Appendix C for your *Password to Prayer*.

Quotable

"It's very easy for us to confuse meekness with the word "weakness." It certainly isn't a virtue that we particularly admire. Yet unless we are meek enough to be teachable, we are not going to be admirable at all." –Elisabeth Elliot

Wednesday • Lesson Three
The Main Course

Today's Passage

Read Proverbs 9:10-12

Proverbs Passkey

The fear of the Lord is the beginning of wisdom, and knowledge of the Holy One is understanding. Proverbs 9:10

Cleaning Your Plate

When I was your age, my family had a tradition of going out to eat every Friday night. We usually went to the same place every week, and I usually ordered the same thing. But one Friday night stands out in my memory because something very unusual happened.

We pulled up in the parking lot ready to enjoy a relaxing dinner. As we headed toward the door of this eatery, however, we noticed that there was a homeless man hanging around. He was obviously looking for a handout. As my family and other diners made their way inside, he was ignored. No one said anything to him, and neither did he say anything to anyone.

We hadn't been in the restaurant long when I noticed the man being seated at a table near us. His waitress was the same one we had. She helped him get situated at his booth and gave him a glass of water. He looked completely out of place in the nice restaurant. His clothes were old and tattered. His long hair desperately needed a good scrubbing. His scraggly beard hung from a thin face that held sad, tired eyes. Carefully, he set his old, shabby hat down on the table next to him and self-consciously attempted to smooth his messy hair. Then he folded his hands respectfully and sat very still as he waited.

Our waitress brought us our meal, and a few minutes after we got our food, he got his. I watched as the waitress brought him a heaping plate of the special that night, spaghetti. I don't remember everything that was said, but as soon as she set his plate before him, he began to curse. The quiet, homeless man suddenly went off like a bomb. He got really angry. What a scene! The waitress began to cry as the man railed at her, pointing at his plate and then at her. Everyone in the restaurant was watching. Within seconds, the manager arrived to investigate the uproar. Sobbing, the waitress fled to the kitchen, and the homeless man was escorted back outside. Soon, a busboy cleared the table, and the restaurant got back to normal.

As we were finishing our meal, our waitress returned to our table.

"Do you need anything else?" she asked. She still had tears in her eyes.

Gently, my mom asked her if she was okay. She nodded, and Mom asked, "What happened?"

"Well," she answered, sniffling, "I saw that bum standing out there. I could tell he didn't have anything, and I felt sorry for him." She explained that she got a free meal, whatever the night's special was, when she worked the dinner shift. So she had checked with the manager and asked him if she could give her free meal that night—the spaghetti dinner—to the homeless man.

The manager agreed. The destitute man was invited in and seated at a table. When the waitress brought him his food, he became angry because *he didn't like spaghetti*. Her kindness and compassion were repaid with cursing and complaining. It was not the reaction she had expected. She had made a sacrifice—gone out on a limb—only to be horribly rejected.

Life is all about sitting down at a table where we do not deserve to be. Not one of us deserved to be born. Humanity was invited to this planet by a loving God who wanted to give us His very best, and His kindness and compassion were repaid with cursing and complaining. When we have the healthy, positive, life-giving fear of God that King Solomon mentions, we sit down at Wisdom's table determined to clean our plate, no matter what happens to be served. Our obedience acknowledges God as the One we serve, not the other way around.

As easily as the beggar was invited in that night, he was just as easily escorted back out. He could have walked away full. He could have walked away with a job as a dishwasher or a busboy! The night was full of opportunity! He walked away empty. May that not be said of us when we dine at Wisdom's table. Let's clean our plates, no matter what is served.

Journaling

☀ Pretend you were the waitress. Write down what you might have expected the homeless man to do and say when you brought him his meal.

_____

_____

_____

_____

_____

_____

_____

_____

_____

☀ Are you going to like everything that is *served* to you in this life? How does God want you to react?

_____

_____

_____

_____

_____

☀ Using what you've learned in this lesson, define the fear of God as though you were explaining it to a first-grader. How would you explain it to a young child?

_____

_____

_____

_____

☀ What is today's date? _____. Check Appendix C for your *Password to Prayer*.

Quotable

"Godly fear stands apart from earthly fears because it has a positive and life-giving influence. Fear in God is an acknowledgment of who we are and who God is. It is putting ourselves in our proper place in the universe by recognizing the power and wisdom of the Creator." –Ed Young, Jr.

Thursday • Lesson Four
Old Mother Hubbard

Today's Passage

Read Proverbs 9:13-18

Proverbs Passkey

"Stolen water is sweet; food eaten in secret is delicious!" But little do they know that the dead are there, that her guests are in the depths of the grave. Proverbs 9:17-18

Secrets of the Cupboard

In the spring of my sixth grade year, cheerleader tryouts were held at my middle school. My best friend Katie* talked me into trying out. It was a dream to be a cheerleader. They were the beautiful, popular girls. When we arrived at tryouts, however, I immediately knew I had made a big mistake. It seemed like everyone except me had swingy hair, a perfect complexion, and athletic coordination. I felt out of place and unsure of myself. I knew from one glance at the competition that I would never make the cut.

As we started going through our routines, I felt stiff and mechanical. The judges watched intently from dead-pan faces, scribbling notes and tapping ball-point pens on the table. Anxiously, I wondered: *Did I smile big enough? Keep my arms straight enough? Jump high enough?*

Most teen girls growing up in America today are concerned with the way they look, which is quite normal and natural. But for some girls, their looks become an area of their lives where they are overly concerned. They become obsessed with controlling the way they look, and that can often lead to the development of eating disorders, like *bulimia* and *anorexia nervosa*, which occur most commonly in teen-aged girls. Most of the time, young women who wrestle with eating disorders are in fact struggling with lives that are out of control due to feelings of abandonment and insecurity. They experience an intense fear of fatness and a distorted body image. The media smothers us in stunning photos of beautiful women with perfect bodies every day. They smile at us from billboards and magazines, along with TV and movie screens. Real women can't measure up to the mirrors and lights that hide models' flaws and make them appear to be without blemish.

Something wonderful has happened since I was a teen: I've learned what God has to say about me, and I've accepted it.

God says that I am fearfully and wonderfully made, whether or not I can do a cartwheel (Psalm 139:14).

God says that I am chosen of God, holy and dearly loved, whether or not I am chosen by a panel of judges (Colossians 3:12).

God says that I am a child of God, and I look like my Father, whether or not I'm having a good hair day (I John 3:1,2).

God says that I am accepted by God because of my faith in Jesus Christ, whether or not I am accepted by other people (Galatians 2:16).

I still have bad hair days, and I still get blemishes. Sometimes I feel fat. Walking into a room full of people I've never met remains somewhat unnerving. And all too often I find myself overly concerned with what earthly judges think: my pastor, my friends, editors, and even complete strangers. *Did I smile big enough? Keep my arms straight enough? Jump high enough?* But the truth is this: It doesn't matter how I feel about me or what other people think. I choose to believe what God says about me—His daughter.

We all need to know that we are not alone. I remember reading the "cut list" on the day after cheerleader tryouts. When I found out I didn't make the cut, I was not alone. In fact, the majority of girls who tried out did not make the squad. We all tried to act like it didn't matter. We saved our tears for after school and spent the rest of the day snubbing our friends who did make the cut. How sad! We were so lost in the pain and deceit of man's rejection that we couldn't be happy for our friends.

In our Father's eyes, we are loved and valued equally. We are His priceless treasures not because we are pretty enough, smart enough, or good enough, but because He created us. No one can take the place you fill in this world. Hurray! That's something to cheer about!

Journaling

♥ Name three things that you like about yourself physically. (Example: My eyes are a pretty color. I have soft hands.)

_____

_____

_____

_____

_____

♥ Name three things that you like about yourself personally. (Example: I'm a good friend. I love helping people.)

_____

_____

_____

_____

💗 Beloved Bible teacher Beth Moore once encouraged a group of mission workers to recite this "pledge of faith" (below), which she uses daily.[33] As you conclude your study of the first nine chapters of Proverbs, you may want to make this part of your morning routine. Copy it on a note card to post on your mirror or beside your bed.

My Pledge of Faith

God is who He says He is.
God can do what He says He can do.
I am who God says I am.
I can do all things through Christ.
God's Word is alive and active in me.

💗 Work on your passage for memorization.

💗 What is today's date? _____. Check Appendix C for your *Password to Prayer*.

Quotable

"Food is just one of the ways we attempt to find satisfaction apart from relationship with our heavenly Father. Some people get drunk every weekend in an effort to quench their thirsty souls. You won't catch me pointing a finger and asking, 'How could you?' I understand. For a while the emptiness inside you seems to go away. Unfortunately, it always comes back." –Lisa Whelchel

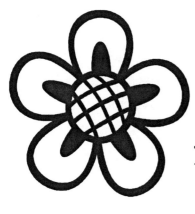

Friday • Lesson Five
Weekending

Today is your day to:

❀ Complete any unanswered questions from this week's lessons.

❀ Read back through Proverbs 9 and your journal entries for this week.

❀ Do some soul-searching about what God is teaching you. Record your thoughts below.

_____

_____

_____

_____

_____

❀ Have you memorized your second Scripture passage? Recite it for a parent. Choose another passage to memorize. Scripture memory should be an ongoing part of your life!

❀ What is today's date? _____. Check Appendix C for your *Password to Prayer*.

❀ Don't forget this week's **EXTRA!** Finish reading the book of Ecclesiastes.

A Note from Rebecca

I am so proud of you for completing this Bible study. I am working on more Bible studies for girls your age. In the meantime, I hope that reading a chapter from Proverbs every day will become your habit. Whatever the day's date, read the corresponding chapter in Proverbs, and continue to use your prayer calendar.

Send me an email at rebecca@rebeccapowell.com and let me know how you liked *Wise Up! Experience the Power of Proverbs.* I would love to hear from you.

With love for you,

Rebecca

To order copies of
Wise Up! Experience the Power of Proverbs,
go to www.rebeccapowell.com.

Appendix A
Brief Bios of Quotable Christians

About Quotables. Each lesson includes a quote from a remarkable Christian. You probably recognized some of the names, but some may have been new to you. Below are brief biographies of the persons behind each Quotable.

Neil T. Anderson is the president emeritus of Freedom in Christ Ministries and a much sought–after speaker on Christ–centered living. Besides the best-selling books *The Bondage Breaker®*, *Victory over the Darkness*, and *Daily in Christ,* he has authored The Bondage Breaker® Series. He has also coauthored many books, including *Getting Anger Under Control* and *Breaking the Bondage of Legalism.*

Mary Kay Ash founded the hugely successful Mary Kay Cosmetics Company in 1963. Her goal was to provide women with an unlimited opportunity for personal and financial success. She used the Golden Rule as her guiding philosophy and encouraged employees and members of her independent sales force to prioritize their lives with God first, family second, and career third. The Company today includes more than 800,000 Independent Beauty Consultants in 37 markets on five continents.

Amy Carmichael was a Christian missionary during the late 1800's and early 1900's whose life remains a model of selfless dedication to the Savior, a life of discipleship and abandonment. She lived for one reason, and that was to make God's love known to those trapped in utter darkness.

Jesus Christ is the Son of God, the source of the Christian religion, and the Savior of the world. Conceived miraculously by his Mother, Mary, through the Holy Spirit, He grew to be received as a great teacher by disciples and common people alike. He preached the redeeming love of God for every person. He was seized by the Romans but turned over to and crucified by Jewish authorities. Rising again on the third day, Christ offers forgiveness of sin and eternal life in Heaven to all who believe He is God's promised Messiah and surrender to His Lordship.

Dr. Don Colbert, M.D. is a board-certified family practitioner. He is the author of several best-selling books, including *What Would Jesus Eat?* Dr. Colbert helps people develop strategies for managing the stresses of life in ways that benefit them physically, emotionally, and spiritually.

Dayna Curry served God as a missionary in Afghanistan. She, along with co-worker Heather Mercer, was arrested by the Taliban government for preaching Christianity and held prisoner for several months. Her devout faith in God sustained her through her ordeal. Learn more about this history-maker in the book, *Prisoners of Hope: The Story of Our Captivity and Freedom in Afghanistan.*

Elisabeth Elliot and her husband Jim served as missionaries to Ecuador in the 1950's. They spent their young lives ministering to a savage tribe, the Quichua Indians, who had never heard of Jesus. Ten months after their only child, Valerie, was born, Jim was killed by the Auca Indians while attempting to take the Gospel to that primitive tribe. Brave Elisabeth continued her work among the Quichuas and later lived and worked among the Aucas, the very people who had killed Jim. Today, Elisabeth is the author of numerous books, including *Passion and Purity*, which details her and Jim's courtship.

Mary Farrar is the author of the book *Choices.* She has served on the staff of Campus Crusade for Christ and has been active in women's ministries. She and her husband Steve are parents of three grown children and live in suburban Dallas.

Billy Graham is a world-renowned author, preacher, and evangelist. He has delivered the Gospel to more people face-to-face than anyone in history, ministering on all seven continents. Some have called him, "America's pastor." Read Rev. Graham's fascinating memoirs in his autobiography, *Just as I Am*.

Joshua Harris is a homeschool graduate. While in his early twenties, he started a revolution with the publication of his book, *I Kissed Dating Good-Bye*. Today he continues to advocate a life of purity. He is a pastor at Covenant Life Church outside Washington, D.C., where he lives with his wife Shannon and their two children.

Vance Havner was a great revival evangelist of the 20th Century. He is one of the most quoted preachers of all time. He was known for frank, straightforward sermons that never sugarcoated the reality of sin or the redemption of the Savior.

Doug Herman is an international speaker and author who has spent over 20 years in youth and family work. Having lost a wife and daughter to AIDS, Doug has emerged from this tragedy strong and true. Currently, Doug speaks to over 250,000 teens and adults yearly about character development, sexual abstinence, and spiritual passion. Learn more about Doug at www.dougherman.com.

Lamont Hiebert is a vocalist and songwriter for the band *Ten Shekel Shirt*. He wrote his first song, "Sing for Joy," when he was 21 years old. *Ten Shekel Shirt* (INO / EPIC Records) merges melodic college rock with Brit pop/rock. Their acoustic driven 2001 debut album, "Much," sold 130,000 units and featured the #1 hit "Ocean." Visit www.tenshekelshirt.com.

Betty Huizenga is the author of *Apples of Gold* and *Appleseeds*. She developed the six-week "Apples of Gold" mentoring program at God's nudging to share what she had learned with younger women.

Jerry B. Jenkins, former vice president for publishing and currently writer-at-large for the Moody Bible Institute of Chicago, is the author of more than 150 books, including the best-selling *Left Behind* series. Learn more at his website, www.jerryjenkins.com.

Martin Luther King, Jr. was an African American Baptist minister who became the predominant leader of the civil rights movement in the United States during the 1950's and 1960's. Dr. King was a gifted communicator who effectively expressed the demands of African Americans for social justice. Thoroughly opposed to violent measures, he led boycotts, sit-ins, and marches, demonstrating a peaceful force for change.

Eric Liddell was an Olympian runner who publicly professed to his faith in Christ. His time in the 100-meter race stood as England's best for thirty-five years. However, during the Paris Olympics in the summer of 1924, the qualifying race for the 100-meter was to be held on a Sunday. Liddell refused to run on what he considered to be a sacred day. Three days later, he took part in the 400-meter race. No one expected him to win, but he did. He won the gold and set a world record. The movie, "Chariots of Fire," chronicles his life.

Heather Mercer served God as a missionary in Afghanistan. She, along with co-worker Dayna Curry, was arrested by the Taliban government for preaching Christianity and held prisoner for several months. Her devout faith in God sustained her through her ordeal. Learn more about this history-maker in the book, *Prisoners of Hope: The Story of Our Captivity and Freedom in Afghanistan.*

Chief Justice Roy Moore is also known as "The Ten Commandments Judge." He has gained national recognition for his courageous defense of the Ten Commandments in the face of career-threatening opposition.

Marilyn Morris is the Founder and President of Aim For Success, the largest provider of sexual abstinence programs in the United States. She is the author of two valuable resources, *ABC's of the Birds and Bees: For Parents of Toddlers to Teens* and *Teens, Sex, and Choices.* Marilyn also publishes a bi-monthly newsletter, "Tips on Encouraging Sexual Abstinence." Visit www.aimforsuccess.org.

Stormie Omartian is a popular writer, speaker, and author of eleven best-selling books including *The Power of a Praying Wife.* Stormie's life goal is to help people find a way out of their pain, lack of fulfillment, or frustration and become all God created them to be.

Saint Paul was one of the most important leaders of early Christianity. A former persecutor of Christians, he met the Lord on the road to Damascus and experienced the transforming power of salvation. He went into missions and founded congregations throughout Asia Minor and southeastern Europe. His letters, called *epistles,* to these newly established churches form a significant part of the New Testament.

Eugene Peterson is a writer and poet. He is Professor Emeritus of Spiritual Theology at Regent College in Vancouver, British Columbia, and served as a pastor for over thirty years. He is the translator of *The Message,* a contemporary rendering of the Bible from the original languages.

Dennis Rainey is the executive director and the cofounder of FamilyLife (a division of Campus Crusade for Christ) and the daily host of the nationally syndicated radio program "FamilyLife Today." Visit www.familylife.com.

Dave Ramsey is a personal money management expert, a popular national radio personality, and the best-selling author of *Financial Peace* and *The Total Money Makeover.* Dave devotes himself full-time to helping ordinary people understand the forces behind their financial distress and how to set things right financially, emotionally, and spiritually. Visit www.daveramsey.com.

Jane Rubietta is a pastor's wife, mother of three, author, and speaker. Jane's passion is to see people's hearts restored by the knowledge of the truth: that God absolutely delights in them, that God is crazy about them, that God would give everything on earth to make sure they know they are loved. Visit www.abounding.org.

Pam Stenzel is a former director of Alpha Women's Center, a counseling center for women undergoing crisis pregnancies. Her experiences there taught her that before teen pregnancy and STD (sexually-transmitted diseases) rates could decline, attitudes of teens toward sex first had to change. Desiring to bring about that change, Pam started speaking nationally full-time and is in great demand both in the U.S.A. and in other countries such as Mexico, Australia, Ireland, and Canada. Pam's book, *Sex has a Price Tag,* is available from her website, www.pamstenzel.com.

Rebecca St. James, a homeschool graduate, is a critically acclaimed Christian music artist, songwriter, and author. Passionate about abstinence, Rebecca proclaims a message of godly living and purity to her audiences. Rebecca's book, *Wait for Me: Rediscovering the Joy of Purity in Romance,* is in its ninth printing. Visit Rebecca's website, www.rsjames.com.

Joni Eareckson Tada is an artist, author, and advocate for the disabled. She is known simply by her first name, Joni, around the world. A diving accident in 1967 left Joni a quadriplegic in a wheelchair. During two years of rehabilitation, she spent long months learning how to paint with a brush between her teeth. Her highly detailed, fine art paintings and prints are collector's items. Joni received a presidential appointment to the National Council on Disability for three and a half years, during which time the Americans with Disabilities Act became law. Visit www.joniandfriends.org.

Lysa TerKeurst is a wife, homeschooling mom, and president of Proverbs 31 Ministries. She is the co-host of the ministry's national radio program, which airs daily across the nation and abroad. Lysa is the author of several books, including *Radically Obedient, Radically Blessed,* and *A Woman's Secret to a Balanced Life* with co-author Sharon Jaynes. Visit www.proverbs31.org.

Rick Warren is the founding pastor of Saddleback Church in Lake Forest, California. He and his wife, Kay, began the church in their home in January 1980, with one family. Today, Saddleback is one of America's largest and best-known churches. Rick is the author of the best-selling book, *The Purpose-Driven Life.*

Lisa Whelchel is a wife, homeschooling mother of three, author, and speaker. She is best known for her role as "Blair" on the 1980's hit sitcom, "The Facts of Life." Visit www.lisawhelchel.com.

Ed Young, Jr. is the Senior Pastor of Fellowship Church in Grapevine, TX. Ed also hosts *Creative Connection*, a nationally syndicated weekday radio program and weekly television program on TBN and Daystar. He is the author of several popular books including *High Definition Living* and *The Creative Marriage.*

Zig Ziglar walked away from a record-setting sales career to help other people become more successful in their personal and professional lives. His name is synonymous with confidence, motivation, and success. A master at motivational speaking, Zig has that rare ability to make audiences comfortable and relaxed, yet completely attentive. As an author, he has written nine books, including the perennial best-selling seller, *See You At The Top,* with over two million copies in print.

Appendix B
Scripturistics!

I didn't realize how much Scripture lay dormant in me until I went to college. One of my new friends, Jennie, was a beautiful, godly young woman who loved the Lord. Jennie had the ability to bring up Scripture in daily conversations. She would quote God's Word as encouragement and advice, never sounding "religious" or "self-righteous" in the process. She was known in our dorm as a friend to be counted on for just the right word at the right time. The girls loved her.

The more I hung around Jennie, the more I began to take on this characteristic. I began to remember Scripture that I had learned as a child. These words became real and personal to me as the Lord, time and again, comforted and instructed me with His truth. Eventually, we Christian girls started a weekly Bible study in our dorm and began sharing Scripture with girls who were hungry for it.

Why Memorize Scripture?

Part of becoming the woman God wants you to be includes memorizing His Word. A high school senior once said that daily Scripture memorization gave her the foundation on which to build her Christian life. She credited memorizing Scripture with increasing her confidence, relieving her worries, and improving her thought life.

Why should you memorize Scripture? Explaining the necessity of memorizing Scripture is much like explaining the reason for eating. We must feed our bodies for nourishment, protection against disease, cleansing, and strength, and we do this out of obedience to God.

Nourishment. Why do you feed your body? Food fuels your body and keeps it functioning. Without food, you would lack the energy you need for living. But you're not just a body. Your body houses your spirit. How do you feed *it*?

Jesus said, "It takes more than bread to stay alive. It takes a steady stream of words from God's mouth."[34] He was talking about your spirit's need for nourishment. Your spirit is fed by God's Word.

Protection against disease. There is an old saying that goes, "My food is my medicine. My medicine is my food." Obviously, if you want your body to operate properly, you must eat the right foods. Part of your body's capacity to function lies in its ability to produce antibodies that fight and protect against disease. With the proper nutrients (food), your body can perform this task with ease.

Numbers of studies have been conducted that show how some foods can help fight and even prevent cancer. Natural herbs and spices are used today to treat medical ailments. Centuries ago, the Native American tribes were known for mixing up all kinds of medicines to treat various illnesses, and today's medical doctors are going back to nature to find remedies for the sick.

Your spirit is diseased and sick because of sin. Sin is sickness that affects everyone. God's Word is a healing balm to soothe the sores left by sin. His Word is a medicine that can take away your sin—providing total healing—through Jesus Christ.

Cleansing. Did you know that certain foods can clean your body on the inside? For example, drinking lots of water each day washes out your digestive system. It cleanses your body of impurities.

The Bible says that Jesus washes the Church with the water of the Word.[35] Knowing God's Word thoroughly can wash the enemy's lies right off your spirit. The enemy, Satan, likes to throw dirt on God's children. "You can't do anything right!" he whispers, like a snake.

However, when you know God's Word, those filthy lies cannot stain you. You can wipe them off by speaking the Truth. "I can do everything through Him who gives me strength!"[36]

To help others. If you didn't eat anything, you would not be able to help anyone. You would become so weak that you would be powerless to do anything. You would be unable to help around the house. You could not do anything to assist your siblings, parents, or grandparents. In fact, other people would be called in to help you. With proper nutrition, your body is strong. You can work. You can serve. You can be a blessing to those who need you.

In the same way, when you know God's Word, you are strong enough to help other people. You can provide them with godly counsel. You can give good advice. You can help them find their way through problems.

Your Father says so. Your parents want you to eat because they know the benefits of good health. They know the role that good foods play in growing strong muscles and bones, and so do you.

Your Heavenly Father, God, wants you to memorize His Word. He wants you to "eat" it—take it in until it becomes a part of you. God told Joshua, "Ponder and meditate on it [Scripture] day and night, making sure you practice everything written in it. Then you'll get where you're going; then you'll succeed."[37] **God's Word is:**

A Revelation

A Signpost

A Life-Map....................

The Direction to Successful Living.

God's Word warns us of danger and directs us to hidden treasure. Otherwise how will we find our way?[38]

Tips for Memorizing Scripture

Memorize one verse at a time. We are memorizing large blocks of Scripture in this Bible study. Let's go at them one verse at a time.

Memorize phrase by phrase. Once you copy down your verse, see if you can break it up into phrases. Underline, use different colored pens or markers, and break up the verse.

Buddy up. Ask a parent, sibling, or friend to memorize the verse with you. Work on the verse together. Hold each other accountable!

Write the verse. Write out the Scripture in your own handwriting on a 3x5 note card, a sticky note, or regular paper. Studies have shown that writing things down helps you remember them.

Read the verse. Listen to yourself as you read the verse aloud several times each day.

Laminate the passage or cover it with clear Contact® paper and post it in the shower. "Sing" the Scripture to a tune you make up!

Listen to the verse. Record yourself reading the verse aloud.

Make an audio tape of different people reading the verse aloud. Ask family members, your pastor and other teachers at church, and your friends to read the verse. Ask them to read the verse slowly, phrase by phrase, so you will have time to repeat after them.

Listen to the tape. Play the tape for your siblings and see if they can guess to whom each voice belongs.

Think about the verse. Post the verse beside your bed. Think about the verse as you drift off to sleep at night.

Put the verse beside your bathroom mirror. Think about what the verse means as you brush your teeth.

Write the verse on a sticky note and put it on the front of one of your school folders. Interchange with the next verse when you have learned the first one.

Do the verse. Researchers have found that an active body promotes an active mind. Get your body moving and your blood pumping, and it will rev up your brain cells!

✸ Make up motions to go along with the verse.

✸ Bounce or dribble a ball while you memorize.

✸ Take a walk with your verse cards in hand.

✸ Try jumping rope while you work on your Scripture.

Create a rewards program. With your parents' approval, come up with a rewards system for your hard work. Draw up a contract and agree that you will only receive the reward when the verse is completely memorized, word for word. (**Please note:** Memorizing Scripture is a reward in and of itself. It is a lasting treasure. However, I don't see anything wrong with rewarding young people for learning the disciplines of hard work and commitment.)

Suggested Scripture Memory Passages

Deuteronomy 30:15-20

1 Samuel 12:20-25

Psalm 1

Psalm 23

Psalm 24

Proverbs 3:1-8

John 15:9-12

Ephesians 4:25-31

Philippians 2:5-11

Philippians 4:10-13

2 Timothy 2:22-26

James 1:19-25

James 2:14-18

Appendix C
Password to Prayer

As you conclude your time of Bible study each day, use these "passwords" as a guide for your own prayers to God. Each prayer is based on a key verse from one of the thirty-one chapters in Proverbs. Coordinate the prayers to the day's date. For example, if today was September 12, you would read the 12th prayer. Tomorrow, you would read the 13th prayer. Pray through these 31 prayers every month. Use these prayers as a springboard to deeper conversations with God.

1 **Dear God,** I praise You. You alone are worthy of my praise. Forgive me for the times that I don't put You first in my life. Thank You for creating me and giving me breath. **Help me to give You my reverence and worship.** May I fear You, Lord, and serve Christ alone.
The fear of the Lord is the beginning of knowledge, but fools despise wisdom and discipline. Proverbs 1:7

2 **Dear God,** I worship You today. You are all powerful. Your angels surround me, guarding me. Please forgive me when I don't trust You to protect me. Thank You for being my Shield and my Defense. **Father, please keep me away from wrong people, wrong places, and dangerous situations.**
For He guards the course of the just and protects the way of His faithful ones. Proverbs 2:8

3 **Dear God,** You are my eternal hope. My heart is Yours. I'm sorry for the times I put myself first instead of You first. I understand that I am to have no other gods before You. Please help me think of You first and acknowledge Your Lordship in everything I do and say.
Trust in the Lord with all your heart and lean not on your own understanding; in all your ways acknowledge Him, and He will make your paths straight. Proverbs 3:5,6

4 **Dear God,** You are the Wonderful Counselor. You are Wisdom and Truth. I admit I make foolish choices sometimes. Please forgive me, Lord. As I get older, my decisions become more important. **Please give me the wisdom of Christ, and teach me to guard my heart.**
Above all else, guard your heart, for it is the wellspring of life. Proverbs 4:23

5 **Dear God,** You are holy, good, and perfect. I'm not like You, Lord, but I want to be. Please help me to stay pure in my thoughts, my words, and my actions. Help me to guard my eyes and my heart. **Give me the strength to wait for my husband and to save my body for him alone.**
For the lips of an adulteress drip honey, and her speech is smoother than oil; but in the end she is bitter as gall, sharp as a double-edged sword. Proverbs 5:3,4

6 **Dear God,** You are the Lord of the harvest. You planned for work to be part of life. I'm sorry for having a bad attitude about my chores and schoolwork sometimes. **Help me to be diligent in my work.** Please develop my gifts and skills so that I can serve You in the work You call me to do.
Go to the ant, you sluggard; consider its ways and be wise! Proverbs 6:6

7 **Dear God,** You are all-knowing. You hold the future in Your hands. I don't know if You plan for me to get married one day, but if You do, that means that my husband is out there somewhere. **Protect his purity, God.** Give him the strength to wait for me.

Many are the victims she has brought down; her slain are a mighty throng. Her house is a highway to the grave, leading down to the chambers of death. Proverbs 7:26,27

8 **Dear God,** Thank You for choosing me. Thank You for choosing to send a Redeemer, Jesus, to save me. Lord, You always make wise choices. **Please teach me how to make good decisions.** I want to choose the very best—the things that will lead me closer to You. Help me in choosing the right direction for my life.

Choose my instruction instead of silver, knowledge rather than choice gold, for wisdom is more precious than rubies, and nothing you desire can compare with her. Proverbs 8:10,11

9 **Dear God,** You know everything. Sometimes I don't care one bit about school, Lord. I don't feel like reading or writing or doing my math. **Please instill in me a love of learning.** Help me to understand that everything I'm learning is helping me to prepare for the life You have planned for me.

Instruct a wise man and he will be wiser still; teach a righteous man and he will add to his learning. Proverbs 9:9

10 **Dear God,** It's amazing to think that Jesus never said a wrong thing. I say wrong things every single day. **I want my mouth to obey You, Lord.** Please help me to say only things that are kind. Help me to build others up and not criticize and insult people, especially my family.

The mouth of the righteous is a fountain of life, but violence overwhelms the mouth of the wicked. Proverbs 10:11

Appendix C

11 **Dear God,** You gave up everything for me, even Your own Son. I can be really stingy sometimes, Lord. **Help me to be a giving person.** Help me to share—not just my things, but also my time, my space, and my attention.

One man gives freely, yet gains even more; another withholds unduly, but comes to poverty. Proverbs 11:24

12 **Dear God,** You have provided standards for living in the Ten Commandments. The Bible is Your instruction book. I don't know why, but I still have trouble sometimes knowing exactly what I should do in certain situations. **I need godly counselors in my life, Lord. And I need You to help me to listen to them.**

The way of a fool seems right to him, but a wise man listens to advice. Proverbs 12:15

13 **Dear God,** You give me everything I need. You are always faithful to me. So Lord, I'm asking: I need some good friends. Please lead me to people who will help me in my Christian walk. Show me other kids my age who want to serve You; lead me to people who are really living out their faith. **Please give me godly friends, and help me to be one, too.**

He who walks with the wise grows wise, but a companion of fools suffers harm. Proverbs 13:20

14 **Dear God,** You can see right through me. You know my innermost thoughts. I pray that You will give me the wisdom of a discerning spirit regarding people, places, and circumstances. Even if it looks good on the outside, it may not be good for me. **Help me know when I am with someone who will bring trouble to my life or when I am somewhere You don't want me to be.**

There is a way that seems right to a man, but in the end it leads to death. Proverbs 14:12

15 **Dear God,** According to You, I am fearfully and wonderfully made. I sure don't feel that way, Lord. Sometimes I feel like my body is out of control. Help me to take care of my body by eating right, exercising every day, and keeping a smile on my face. **Help me to remember my body is Your temple.**

A cheerful look brings joy to the heart, and good news gives health to the bones. Proverbs 15:30

16 **Dear God,** Why do I act this way? I don't mean to talk back, and I don't mean to be rude to my family. I don't know what comes over me, Lord. At the time, the things I say and do seem right. Then I realize that I shouldn't have, and I wish I didn't. **Please give me greater self-control.**

Better a patient man than a warrior, a man who controls his temper than one who takes a city. Proverbs 16:32

17 **Dear God,** Without Your forgiveness, I would be lost. Father, forgive me when I am slow to forgive others—when I hold on to hurts. I end up getting more hurt that way. **Please help me to live a life of ongoing forgiveness, not necessarily because I feel like it, but because forgiveness is what You ask me to do.**

He who covers over an offense promotes love, but whoever repeats the matter separates close friends. Proverbs 17:9

18 **Dear God,** You are my best friend. You loved me enough to die for me. Your Word says that a friend loves all the time. I want to learn to be a good friend. Please help me to understand what that means. Forgive me for my selfishness and for not putting others first. Help me to be patient and kind and fun to be around. **Help me to be the kind of friend others are looking for.**

A man of many companions may come to ruin, but there is a friend who sticks closer than a brother. Proverbs 18:24

19 **Dear God,** Even Jesus had to obey His mom and dad. I'm sure that He did it much more cheerfully than I do at times. It is so hard sometimes! They have opinions about everything, Lord. I want to please them, but they sure do ask a lot from me! **Please help me to mind my parents, to love them, and to honor them with my respectful submission.**

He who obeys instructions guards his life, but he who is contemptuous of his ways will die. Proverbs 19:16

20 **Dear God,** Drugs and alcohol are a trap. They look like a party, but they are a funeral. Instead of living, people just start dying when they get involved with drugs. I don't want to miss out on a job, a home, and a family. I pray that I will never fall for that trap. **Please, Lord, guard my life from the destruction of addictions.**

Wine is a mocker and beer a brawler; whoever is led astray by them is not wise. Proverbs 20:1

21 **Dear God,** I praise You, O Lord. You alone are worthy. God, I'm sorry. Today I just got tired of being good. I got tired of trying. Now I'm miserable. Help me to run this race called life with a steadfast determination to make it to the finish line. Help me to keep putting one foot in front of the other, whether I feel like it or not. **Keep me in hot pursuit of righteousness and love.**

He who pursues righteousness and love finds life, prosperity, and honor. Proverbs 21:21

22 **Dear God,** Yours is the Name above all Names. I want to be known for having a good name, too, Lord. In many ways, it is important what others think about me. I want to be known for being a Christian, Lord. That sounds pretty simple, but I don't think it's going to be easy. **Guard my reputation, Lord. May my actions only bring you glory, never shame.**

A good name is more desirable than great riches; to be esteemed is better than silver or gold. Proverbs 22:22

23 **Dear God,** You are so great! Let me thank You today for everything I can think of. Maybe that will help me quit wanting so much more. I keep asking Mom and Dad for stuff; it's like I'm out of control! **Teach me to be content with what You provide.**

Do not wear yourself out to get rich; have the wisdom to show restraint. Proverbs 23:4

24 **Dear God,** I'm so glad that You created families. I wonder what mine will be like. I know that no matter what, You have a good plan for my life. Please show me the path I am to take, and help me to follow every step as You lead me. **Whether I am single or married, childless or managing a house full of kids, please bless my future home.**

By wisdom a house is built, and through understanding it is established; through knowledge its rooms are filled with rare and beautiful treasures. Proverbs 24:3,4

25 **Dear God,** The more I learn about You, Lord, the more it seems You tell me to do the opposite of what I want to do! Love my enemies? Pray for the people who mistreat me? It's really hard to treat other people the way that You would treat them. **May I live by the Golden Rule,** Lord, because the truth is, that's the way I want others to treat me: with grace, understanding, and love.

If your enemy is hungry, give him food to eat; if he is thirsty, give him water to drink. In doing this, you will heap burning coals on his head, and the Lord will reward you. Proverbs 25:21,22

26 **Dear God,** I can't do anything without You, Lord. And yet I find myself many times thinking that I can. I can be nice. I can be respectful. I can have self-control. But I can't. Not without Your help. I don't want to be full of myself, Lord. I want to be full of You. **Teach me true humility, Lord, and may I not be prideful.**

Do you see a man wise in his own eyes? There is more hope for a fool than for him. Proverbs 26:12

---

27 **Dear God,** I want my friends and everyone that I meet to know that I am a Christian. I want them to see Jesus all over me. I don't just want Him in my heart, Lord. I want Him in my smile, my laughter, my compassion, and my attitude. **May my heart reflect the One who lives there, Jesus Christ.** And may He shine through my thoughts, my words, and my deeds.

As water reflects a face, so a man's heart reflects the man. Proverbs 27:19

28 **Dear God,** Please bring to my mind now the sins that I may have pushed toward the back of my brain. Help me to recall the sins that I haven't asked forgiveness for. And Lord, even if it might be terribly difficult, please show me if there is anyone whose forgiveness I need to ask. Have I hurt someone and not apologized? On the flip side, is there someone with whom I am upset, someone I need to forgive? It doesn't matter if that person has asked my forgiveness. I need to forgive simply to be right with You. **Search my heart—reveal my foolish ways.**

He who conceals his sins does not prosper, but whoever confesses and renounces them finds mercy. Proverbs 28:13

29 **Dear God,** Sometimes I am afraid of what people will think about me. I try too hard to be who I think others are expecting me to be. That's not right. You made me to be Your own special treasure. You are the One Who loves me most. You created my personality and the way I am. **Help me to be myself.** I want to be a God-pleaser, not a people-pleaser.

Fear of man will prove to be a snare, but whoever trusts in the Lord is kept safe. Proverbs 29:25

30 **Dear God,** Sometimes I just don't feel like picking up my Bible. I'm sorry, Lord. Would You please make it be like candy to me? Make it something that I just can't resist! Help me to love it more, and lead me to study it with my whole heart. I know there are great truths and riches to be found in the Bible. **May I desire the wonders found only in Your Word.**

Every word of God is flawless; He is a shield to those who take refuge in Him. Proverbs 30:5

31 **Dear God,** I want to fear the Lord, and serve Him alone. I want to be able to provide godly counsel and words of righteous wisdom to my friends when they're in trouble. I want other people to know that Jesus really is the only way to God. And Lord, I want to tell people that with love. I want to share Your love. Your love and Your light shining through me will make me beautiful, and others will see Jesus in my life. **Make me the woman You want me to be.**

Charm is deceptive, and beauty is fleeting; but a woman who fears the Lord is to be praised. Proverbs 31:30

About the Author

Rebecca Ingram Powell is a wife and homeschooling mom. She received a Bachelor of Arts degree in English with a minor in Speech Communications, graduating magna cum laude with University Honors from Middle Tennessee State University. She is the author of *Baby Boot Camp: Basic Training for the First Six Weeks of Motherhood* and writes the popular monthly column, "A Mom's Life" for *ParentLife* magazine. Rebecca and her husband Rich were college sweethearts and today live in a suburb of Nashville, Tennessee, with their three children, Danya, David, and Derek.

Rebecca enjoys speaking to women's groups, homeschooling moms, and of course, teens. She is approachable and real as she spends time with your group, confronting real-life problems and clearly presenting practical solutions from God's Word. Topics include: "The Virtuous Woman: Her Habits, Home, and Heart," "Intentional Intimacy: God's Invitation to Meet with Him," "Wise Up! Five Things to Know about Your Adolescent Daughter," and "Where are They Now? Life After High School."

For more information on booking Rebecca for speaking engagements, please visit www.rebeccapowell.com.

End Notes

1. This video is available from Nantucket Publishing, on the web at www.unshackled.com, or call toll-free: 1.800.430.7719. Email Nantucket Publishing: Nantucket@yahoo.com.

2. Names throughout this curriculum have been changed. Pseudonyms are denoted by an asterisk (*).

3. 1 Corinthians 15:33, *GOD'S WORD*.

4. Galatians 6:8, *The Message*

5. Anderson, Neil. Spiritual Discernment. The Faithful Hope Reading Room. <http://www.faithfulhope.com/readingroom/item.cfm?doc_id=7998>.

6. TerKeurst, Lysa, and Sharon Jaynes. A Woman's Secret to a Balanced Life. Eugene, OR: Harvest House, 2004.

7. Naber, John. John Naber's Simple Advice ... 'No Deposit, No Return.' 21 April 2004. <http://www.olympic-usa.org/132_18776.htm>.

8. Matthew 7:13, *The Message*

9. Heb. 11:1, NIV

10. *The Message*

11. Stenzel, Pam. Sex has Price Tag. (adapted) <http://www.prolife.com/stenzel.htm>.

12. *The Message*

13. Matthew 12:36, *The Message*.

14. Merriam-Webster Online Dictionary. <http://www.merriamwebster.com>.

15. This story is adapted from a legend.

16. Mercer & Curry bring lessons of Afghan imprisonment to SBC, June 12, 2002. *By Karen L. Willoughby* <http://www.bpnews.net>

17. James 1:13-14, NIV

18. I Peter 5:8, NIV

19. Morris, Marilyn. "He Said, She Said." <u>Tips for Encouraging Sexual Abstinence.</u> January, 2004: 1-2.

20. Doug is paraphrasing Luke 7:23.

21. Proverbs 8:4-11, *The Message*

22. Excerpted from "Searching for Pleasure" by Billy Graham, DECISION August 2003, © 2003 Billy Graham Evangelistic Association, used by permission, all rights reserved.

23. 1 Kings 4:30, NIV

24. Cf. Ecclesiastes 1:2

25. Ecclesiastes 2:10, NIV

26. Cf. Ecclesiastes 1:14

27. Matthew 27:40, NIV

28. Colossians 2:3, NIV

29. Matthew 12:42, NIV

30. Ecclesiastes 12:13-14, NIV

31. Daniel 1:4 NLT

32. Ecclesiastes 1:9, NIV

33. Roten, Manda. "Beth Moore: Pour out your life & believe God for the impossible." BP News. 30 Oct. 2003. <http://www.bpnews.net/bpnews.asp?ID=16966>.

34. Matthew 4:4, *The Message*

35. Ephesians 5:26

36. Philippians 4:13, NIV

37. Joshua 1:8b, *The Message*

38. Psalm 19:11, *The Message*

To order additional copies of

WiSe Up!

Please visit www.rebeccapowell.com

Or have your credit card ready and call:

Pleasant Word
1-877-421-READ (7323)

LaVergne, TN USA
03 February 2010
171873LV00001B/3/A